# Benchmark Assessment

Level 5

## Blackline Masters

Doug Fuchs

Lynn Fuchs

Columbus, Ohio

SRAonline.com

Printed in the United States of America.

Send all inquiries to this address:
SRA/McGraw-Hill
4400 Easton Commons
Columbus, OH 43219-6188

ISBN: 978-0-07-617647-2
MHID: 0-07-617647-9

2 3 4 5 6 7 8 9 QPD 13 12 11 10 09 08

The McGraw-Hill Companies

# Table of Contents


**Introduction** . . . . . . . . . . . . . . . . . . . . . . . . . . . . iv

## Benchmark Test 1

**Group Assessments** . . . . . . . . . . . . . . . . . . . . . 2

**Oral Fluency** . . . . . . . . . . . . . . . . . . . . . . . . . . 16

**Writing Prompt** . . . . . . . . . . . . . . . . . . . . . . . 19

## Benchmark Test 2

**Group Assessments** . . . . . . . . . . . . . . . . . . . . . 20

**Oral Fluency** . . . . . . . . . . . . . . . . . . . . . . . . . . 34

## Benchmark Test 3

**Group Assessments** . . . . . . . . . . . . . . . . . . . . . 37

**Oral Fluency** . . . . . . . . . . . . . . . . . . . . . . . . . . 51

## Benchmark Test 4

**Group Assessments** . . . . . . . . . . . . . . . . . . . . . 54

**Oral Fluency** . . . . . . . . . . . . . . . . . . . . . . . . . . 68

**Writing Prompt** . . . . . . . . . . . . . . . . . . . . . . . 71

## Benchmark Test 5

**Group Assessments** . . . . . . . . . . . . . . . . . . . . . 72

**Oral Fluency** . . . . . . . . . . . . . . . . . . . . . . . . . . 86

## Benchmark Test 6

**Group Assessments** . . . . . . . . . . . . . . . . . . . . . 89

**Oral Fluency** . . . . . . . . . . . . . . . . . . . . . . . . . . 103

## Benchmark Test 7

**Group Assessments** . . . . . . . . . . . . . . . . . . . . . 106

**Oral Fluency** . . . . . . . . . . . . . . . . . . . . . . . . . . 120

**Writing Prompt** . . . . . . . . . . . . . . . . . . . . . . . 123

**Benchmark Test Answer Sheets** . . . . 124

**Teacher Records** . . . . . . . . . . . . . . . . . . 145

# *Imagine It!* Benchmark Assessment

***Benchmark Assessment*** forms the backbone of the ***Imagine It!*** assessment system. The ***Benchmark Assessment*** consists of seven evaluations that are administered periodically throughout the school year. The first Benchmark test is administered at the beginning of the year, and subsequent Benchmarks are administered at the end of each unit.

***Imagine It! Benchmark Assessment*** differs from traditional classroom tests in two important ways. First, each Benchmark samples skills from the entire year-long curriculum, rather than sampling skills taught in the most recent unit. Second, all of the Benchmarks within a grade have the same format, sample the same content, and are of equivalent difficulty. Thus, improving scores on the Benchmark Assessments over the course of the year indicate students' increasing mastery of the grade-level curriculum. (For a more detailed explanation of the rationale of the structure of the Benchmark Assessments, see the ***Imagine It!*** Professional Development Guide to Assessment.)

# Components of Benchmark Assessments

The Benchmark Assessments have three major components:

- The 100-Point Skills Battery
- Oral Fluency
- Expository Writing

## The 100-Point Skills Battery

This component samples skills from strands within the grade level curriculum. Reading comprehension, vocabulary, grammar, usage and mechanics, and spelling comprise the skills battery in Level 5. Each strand has been assigned a weight in accordance with its importance in the curriculum to reach the total of 100 points. The table below shows the strands in Level 5, the number of items in each strand, the weight given to each item within a strand, and the setting in which the assessment of the strand is administered.

**Level 5**

| Strand | # Items | Total weight | Format | Setting |
|---|---|---|---|---|
| Comprehension | 20 | 40 | Multiple Choice | Group |
| Vocabulary | 10 | 30 | Multiple Choice | Group |
| Grammar, Usage, and Mechanics | 10 | 20 | Multiple Choice | Group |
| Spelling | 10 | 10 | Multiple Choice | Group |

## Oral Fluency

The Fluency portion of the ***Benchmark Assessment*** is a direct measure of students' reading fluency. It also serves as a general, overall indicator of a student's reading competence. For example, students who score poorly when reading text aloud in a fixed time are the same students who have poor decoding skills, whose ability to recognize words automatically is inadequate, who have limited vocabularies, and who have difficulty understanding what they read. In Level 5 there are two fluency options from which to choose:

- Individually administered oral fluency passages
- Group-administered MAZE passages

### Individually Administered Passages

Students will have one minute to read aloud the Oral Fluency passage for each Benchmark test, although they are not expected to complete the passage before the minute has passed. You will time each student, noting any errors the student makes and calculating his or her correct words per minute (WPM) and accuracy rate from the instructions on page x of the introduction. Because this portion of the Benchmark Assessment must be individually administered, you will need to allot at least 2 minutes for each student in your classroom so that each student has time to read to you and so that you have enough time to transition from student to student.

### Group-Administered MAZE Passages

If you prefer to administer a group fluency assessment, a MAZE passage is provided. This passage has the same text as the oral fluency passage. However, students will not be reading the MAZE passage aloud. Instead, they will have three minutes to read silently and choose the correct words to complete the sentences. Like the Oral Fluency Assessment, students are not expected to complete the MAZE passage before the allotted time has passed.

**NOTE:** Students should be assessed using **either** the Oral Fluency Assessment **or** the MAZE Passage, but not **both**.

## Expository Writing

A Writing Assessment is included with the first, fourth, and seventh Benchmark Assessments at this grade level. For each Writing Assessment, make a copy of the prompt and make sure students have paper and writing materials. These prompts for expository writing are similar to the type of prompt found in high-stakes tests. A checklist is provided to help students focus their work. Students will be graded using the Four Point Rubrics for Expository Writing found on page 145.

Students who fall below cutoffs in the writing should be monitored during their classroom writing assignments. If a student's writing shows little or no improvement, do not wait until the next Benchmark to intervene. Provide the necessary support to ensure the student begins writing cohesive text in a grade-level appropriate manner.

# Purposes of Benchmark Assessments

The Benchmark Assessments serve three major purposes in the classroom:

- Screening
- Progress Monitoring
- Diagnosis

## Screening

Screening is the process of measuring all students in a class to identify the subset of students who, without special attention, are in danger of scoring poorly on the end-of-the year high-stakes tests and of long-term reading failure. Cutoff scores for the Benchmark Assessments are provided below. At the beginning of the year, and then periodically throughout the year, any student who falls below the cutoff score on the 100-Point Skills Battery, Fluency Assessment, and Expository Writing Assessment should be considered for intervention. That student's progress should be closely monitored through weekly fluency assessments.

***100-Point Skills Battery***

| Benchmark 1 | Benchmark 2 | Benchmark 3 | Benchmark 4 | Benchmark 5 | Benchmark 6 | Benchmark 7 |
|---|---|---|---|---|---|---|
| 20 | 30 | 42 | 54 | 66 | 78 | 90 |

***Fluency Cutoffs–Oral Reading Fluency***

| Benchmark 1 | Benchmark 2 | Benchmark 3 | Benchmark 4 | Benchmark 5 | Benchmark 6 | Benchmark 7 |
|---|---|---|---|---|---|---|
| 85 | 98 | 112 | 126 | 140 | 154 | 168 |

***Fluency Cutoffs–MAZE***

| Benchmark 1 | Benchmark 2 | Benchmark 3 | Benchmark 4 | Benchmark 5 | Benchmark 6 | Benchmark 7 |
|---|---|---|---|---|---|---|
| 12 | 13 | 14 | 15 | 16 | 17 | 18 |

***Expository Writing Cutoffs***

| Benchmark 1 | Benchmark 2 | Benchmark 3 | Benchmark 4 | Benchmark 5 | Benchmark 6 | Benchmark 7 |
|---|---|---|---|---|---|---|
| 11 | N/A | N/A | 13 | N/A | N/A | 15 |

## Progress Monitoring

Because each of the Benchmark Assessments is constant in difficulty and format, they provide a means for measuring the progress of all students in a classroom over the course of the academic year. Improving total scores on the Benchmark Assessments indicate a student's increasing mastery of the language arts curriculum.

## Diagnosis

Because each of the segments of the Benchmark Assessments provides a separate score in each of the strands of the curriculum, the assessments can be used to identify the specific curriculum areas that are strengths or weaknesses for a student or across a classroom.

If students score below the cutoff for any Benchmark Assessment, use one or more of the following options to help students get back on track:

- **Reteach**—use this with students who need extra help with comprehension; spelling; vocabulary; and grammar, usage, and mechanics
- **Intervention**—assign this to students who need more intensive help with comprehension; spelling; vocabulary; grammar, usage, and mechanics; oral fluency; and writing
- **Workshop Planner Activities**—have students work on these activities to improve their comprehension; spelling; vocabulary; oral fluency; and grammar, usage, and mechanics skills

- **Leveled Readers (Approaching Level)**—allow students to read these leveled books to improve their comprehension, vocabulary, and fluency skills
- **Leveled Science Readers (Approaching Level)**—distribute these books for students to read to improve their comprehension, vocabulary, and fluency skills
- **Leveled Social Studies Readers (Approaching Level)**—hand out these books to students to read in order to improve their comprehension, vocabulary, and fluency skills
- **Workshop Kit**—utilize the activities in this kit to give students extra practice with comprehension; vocabulary; grammar, usage, and mechanics; and oral fluency skills

## Attributes of Benchmark Assessment

The Benchmark Assessments differ from traditional tests because each Benchmark Assessment tests skills from the entire year-long curriculum; by contrast, many classroom tests address only the skills or content most recently taught. This means that the Benchmark Assessments at the beginning of the year may be very difficult for some students. It is important for both you and your students to understand that the Benchmark Assessments are designed in a way that permits students to show growth (i.e., to improve or obtain increasingly higher scores) over the school year, as you teach them the important skills and strategies incorporated within ***Imagine It!*** On the 100-Point Skills Battery, for example, students are not expected to answer every question correctly at the beginning of the year. The hope is that by the end of the year, students will answer all questions correctly on the 100-Point Skills Battery. On the Fluency section, a similar situation exists. Students are not expected to complete the entire assessment in the time limit at the beginning or even at the end of the year. The Fluency time limit is deliberately set to reduce the possibility that students will complete the task before time is up.

The Benchmark Assessments provide unique assessment opportunities in the classroom, including the ability to monitor students' progress through the consistency of the tests and the ability to prepare students for high-stakes tests.

### Consistency

The Benchmark Assessments are designed to be equivalent in format, content, and difficulty. This equivalency is the key to monitoring a student's progress over the course of the school year. It is equally important for you to maintain consistency as you administer the Benchmark Assessments over the course of the school year. For example, students' performance on tests may vary depending on the time of day or the day of the week. Therefore, it is important to administer each Benchmark Assessment over the course of the year on the same day of the week, at the same time of day, and in the same classroom or space. Also, it is important to follow the time limits for each strand in order to maintain consistency over the course of the school year in the amount of time students have to work on the assessments.

### Preparation for High-Stakes Tests

An added benefit to the Benchmark Assessments is that they should help students and teachers prepare for end-of-the-year high stakes tests. Most importantly, the scores on the Benchmark Assessments provide the information you need to identify which students need additional attention on a certain portion of the curriculum. In addition, the Benchmark Assessments may also provide an opportunity for students to practice taking tests in a formal setting. These assessments are similar in format to many high-stakes tests in that they sample a variety of skills, have several component sections, are timed, and have similar question formats. With the administration of each Benchmark Assessment, you have the opportunity to help students practice their test-taking skills for end-of-the-year testing.

On the day before the administration of a Benchmark Assessment, remind students to get a good night's sleep and eat a good breakfast, just as they would before end-of-the-year testing. On the day of the assessment, set up the classroom in the same way as will be done for high-stakes testing by separating desks, using student "offices," and so on. This will help your students become accustomed to this form of test taking.

After students have taken an assessment and you have scored it, you can use it for discussion purposes. Because specific questions are not repeated across Benchmark Assessments, you can use these questions to highlight certain skills or to discuss strategies for attacking a question or general test-taking strategies.

# Administration of Benchmark Assessments

## Time Limits

Time limits for each 100-Point Battery test are as follows:

| Strand | Time Limit |
|---|---|
| Comprehension | 20 minutes |
| Vocabulary | 10 minutes |
| Grammar, Usage, and Mechanics | 10 minutes |
| Spelling | 10 minutes |

## Test-Taking Procedure

Administer the tests without aiding the students in any academic way. While logistical questions may be answered ("Is this the right page?" or "Do I have a page missing?"), you should not answer questions such as "What is this word?" or "What am I supposed to do?" that may give the student an advantage academically.

Assemble the pages of the group administration part of the Benchmark test that you are giving and make a copy for each student. Staple or clip the pages together for each student, making sure that the sections of the Benchmark are in this order: Comprehension; Vocabulary; Grammar, Usage and Mechanics; and Spelling.

Once you are ready to administer the 100-Point Battery of the Benchmark test, distribute a copy of it to each student. Be sure all students have a copy of the test. Once they do, say:

*Please take your pencil and fill in the information at the top of the front page of the booklet. Today's date is on the board. Please write neatly. When you have finished, put down your pencil and wait for my instructions.*

Circulate around the room to be sure students fill in this information completely and accurately. Once they have, say:

*You will be taking the* comprehension *part of the test first. Read all the directions completely as you come to them. You will be given* **20** *minutes to complete this section of the test. I will write '5 minutes' on the board when there are five minutes left. This section of the test will end when you come to a "STOP" sign. When I say "Time," that means this section is over. You should put down your pencil immediately and wait for my directions.*

Ask students if they understand the process. Then say:

*As you read and answer the questions, be sure to choose only one answer for each question. Be sure that you fill in the circle for each answer completely. If you erase any marks, make sure that you erase them completely. Do not look ahead or mark anything on any other section except this section.*

*If you finish before the time is up, you may check your work. Be sure that your answers are clearly marked and that all unwanted marks are erased completely.*

*If you have questions, you may raise your hand and I will come to your desk. However, I cannot tell you answers, give you hints about answers, or explain test questions.*

*Do you have any questions now? You may begin.*

When time is up for the section, say:

*The time is up for the comprehension section. Please put down your pencils.*

Continue with the remaining sections of the benchmark test in the same fashion, changing directions in relation to time limit. Add the following directions so that students understand what is expected of them: *When you reach the "STOP" sign, you may look back over your answers in this section. However, you cannot go back and work on sections that have been completed earlier.*

When the Benchmark test is complete, collect all the tests. Allow time for a short break before administering Fluency and/or Writing assessments.

## Individual Passage Reading

You will find oral fluency assessments for each Benchmark test.

Make a copy for yourself of the Oral Fluency Assessment for each student you will be assessing. Provide students with a copy of the passage. The teacher and student versions follow each other in the ***Benchmark Assessment*** book. Be sure you have a pen or pencil, a stopwatch or other timer, and extra paper to record any observations. Record the student's name, the date of the assessment, and the results of the assessment.

Have the student sit comfortably at a table with you. Seat yourself and the student so that you can mark the assessment unobtrusively without distracting the student.

**Say:** *Here is a selection I would like you to read aloud for me. I am going to listen to you read and take some notes. The notes I take will help me learn how well you can read. Read the selection carefully and do your best. Are you ready?* (Check to be sure the student is ready.) *You may begin now.*

Start the timer or watch as the student begins to read. You may pronounce any proper nouns with which the student is unfamiliar. Do not count these words as errors. At the end of one minute place a bracket ( ] ) at the end of the last word the student reads.

The following guidelines will help you score the assessment accurately and consistently.

- Self-correcting should not be counted as an error.
- Repeating the same mistake should be counted as only one error.
- Hesitating for more than five seconds—at which point you would have provided the word—should count as an error.
- Draw a line through any word that is misread. Count this as an error. If possible, note the type of error (misreading short *a* as short *e*, reading *get* as *jet*, and so on).
- Words the student omits should be counted as errors, even if you prompt the student.
- Indicate with a caret extra words that have been inserted. If possible, write the inserted word. Count insertions as errors.
- Draw an arrow between words that have been reversed. Count these as one error.
- Students might repeat words on occasion. Do not count this behavior as an error.
- Complete the Reading Rate and Accuracy box after a student has read for the minute. This will give you the student's correct words read per minute (WPM) and the student' accuracy rate.
- Enter the student's WPM at the top of the page. Then transfer that number to the appropriate Benchmark Assessment Record and note whether the student has reached the expected fluency cutoff.
- Next examine the student's accuracy rate. Reading accuracy should remain constant or gradually increase within a grade and between grades, until it stabilizes at ninety percent or higher. You may find it helpful to compare a student's accuracy rate after each administration to ensure that it remains constant or increases.
- Complete the Reading Fluency scale at the bottom of your Oral Fluency Assessment page. These qualitative measures indicate your subjective judgment of how the student compares with other students who are reading at grade level.
- Note the types of errors a student makes. Track if similar errors occur or are corrected as the student progresses through the Benchmarks.

## Group MAZE Passages

Make a copy of the MAZE passage, ask students to write their name and date at the top of the page, and say the following:

*The story you are going to read has some places where you need to choose the correct word. You will read the story, and whenever you come to three words that are in brackets and boldfaced, you will choose the word that belongs in the story. Choose the correct word by circling the answer. You have three minutes to work on this passage. Do not worry if you do not finish in the time given. Is everyone ready? You may begin now.*

After time is up, collect the papers. Compare student responses to the answer sheet provided for the MAZE passage. Write students' scores on their papers and on the appropriate Benchmark Assessment Record. Note whether students have reached the expected MAZE fluency cutoff.

## Time Management

The Benchmark Assessments are administered using a time frame that matches content and time expectations found in high-stakes testing. As such, the expectations placed on your students are both realistic and demanding. In the early Benchmark tests, you will find that students will not finish sections or the entire test on time. If this behavior continues as Benchmark tests progress, use your professional judgment as to whether maintaining consistency of time limits is adversely affecting your students' reaction to the Benchmark Assessment. If you believe this is the case, do allow for some leeway on the time. However, do not add so much time that the data you gather is no longer an accurate representation of student achievement. For example, adding ten minutes to the comprehension will affect your knowledge of whether students can quickly and accurately access and process grade-appropriate text.

# Teacher Records

Benchmark Assessment offers a variety of means to mark and note student progress. Initially, you should grade the Benchmark tests section-by-section and list the total score on the first page of the test after the student name. Use the Answer Sheets located on pages 124–144 to assist you. You will find it beneficial to store each student's pages and test booklets in a folder or binder and then transfer that information to the Benchmark Assessment Record and the Benchmark Tracking Chart.

## Benchmark Assessment Record

A Benchmark Assessment Record page is provided for each test at the back of this book. The spaces following the student's name allow for the recording of student scores in each assessment strand; the total scores achieved in the 100-Point Skills Battery; fluency scores; writing scores; and whether students have reached the necessary cutoff points.

The Benchmark Assessment Record provides an easy way to record student growth across the year.

## Benchmark Tracking Chart

Duplicate this page for each student. The cutoffs for each 100-Point Battery are listed. Map student numbers on this chart using data from the test booklets and/or the Benchmark Assessment Record. Plotting student scores will give you a quick visual appreciation of progress, standing, and student trends. You can create a similar page to chart students' fluency numbers, if you wish.

Name ______________________ Date __________ Score __________

## Comprehension

**Read the following story. Then answer questions 1–10 relating to the story. You may look back at the story to find the answers.**

Jamie dragged her feet, hoping she would arrive at school at the last minute. The fifth graders were taking turns making the announcements each morning before school. This month her class had its turn. Students were chosen in alphabetical order. Art was the only person ahead of her. He was out sick yesterday and Mr. Martin had asked Jamie to replace Art if he was out sick again today.

Although she had nodded in agreement, Jamie was scared. She could not imagine talking to the whole school, fearing that her voice would come out squeaky and that she would not be able to think. She would never live it down.

If she were late, Mr. Martin would move on to the next person, at least that is what Jamie hoped. Maybe he would even skip her altogether. She dawdled outside the school entrance until it was almost time for the final bell, and then she hurried to her classroom, making it just as the bell rang. To her relief, Art was sitting at his desk. She thought she was saved.

"Jamie," Mr. Martin said, "they're waiting for you in the office."

"But I wasn't late," Jamie stammered.

Mr. Martin chuckled. "You're not in trouble. It's your turn for announcements." When Jamie looked at Art, Mr. Martin said, "Art lost his voice, so you'll need to take his place. Don't worry. You'll do a fine job."

## Comprehension (continued)

Mr. Martin's words echoed in Jamie's head as she hurried down the hall. How could she do an excellent job if she was too scared to speak?

The school secretary smiled as Jamie walked into the office. "Good, you're here," she said and handed Jamie a paper. "It's written out, so all you have to do is read the announcements. Forget everyone else. Just act as if there's no one here but you and me."

Jamie bit her lip. How could she forget the whole school was listening? Nonetheless, she cleared her throat and started. Her voice shook a little at first, but she was usually a good reader, and her nervousness passed. She concentrated on the paper, pretending she was alone in her bedroom, reading the words aloud. In a few minutes, it was over.

"Thank you, Jamie," the secretary said. "You did a beautiful job."

Jamie smiled as she walked down the hall to her classroom. Mr. Martin was right; she had done a fine job.



GO ON

## Comprehension (continued)

**1.** This story is mostly about

Ⓐ a girl who was afraid to do announcements.

Ⓑ a boy who missed school because he was sick.

Ⓒ a teacher who made students read the announcements.

Ⓓ a boy who had a sore throat and could not talk.

**2.** Why does Jamie get to school at the last minute?

Ⓐ She does not want to meet Art in the hall.

Ⓑ She does not want to do the announcements.

Ⓒ She forgot her homework and has to get it.

Ⓓ She misses the bus and has to walk to school.

**3.** Why does Jamie not want to do the announcements?

Ⓐ She does not think it is her turn yet.

Ⓑ She does not read very well.

Ⓒ She is nervous about it.

Ⓓ She will miss her favorite class.

**4.** Why is Jamie glad to see Art at school?

Ⓐ She thinks he will do announcements.

Ⓑ She has been worried about Art's health.

Ⓒ She and Art have plans after school that day.

Ⓓ She wants someone to sit with at lunch.

**5.** Why does Mr. Martin tell Jamie to go to the office?

Ⓐ She is late for school that morning.

Ⓑ He wants her to take a note to the principal.

Ⓒ She needs to take Art's place.

Ⓓ There is a phone call for her in the office.

## Comprehension (continued)

**6.** What advice does the school secretary give Jamie?

Ⓐ Pretend you are in your bedroom.

Ⓑ Do not look at the pages when you read.

Ⓒ Pretend no one else is listening.

Ⓓ Speak loudly and clearly.

**7.** What does Jamie do before she starts to read?

Ⓐ She looks over the paper.

Ⓑ She clears her throat.

Ⓒ She reads aloud to herself.

Ⓓ She turns on the mike.

**8.** From this story, you can tell that Mr. Martin

Ⓐ is very strict with his students.

Ⓑ worries that his students might fail.

Ⓒ wants his students to pay attention.

Ⓓ tries to encourage his students.

**9.** What happens to Jamie after she starts reading?

Ⓐ Her voice gets high and squeaky.

Ⓑ Her nervousness passes.

Ⓒ Her hands shake badly.

Ⓓ Her eyesight is blurry.

**10.** How might Jamie have felt once the announcements were over?

Ⓐ relieved, but proud

Ⓑ sad and frightened

Ⓒ glad, but worried

Ⓓ uncertain and nervous

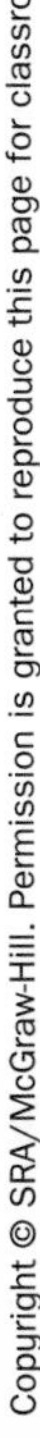


GO ON

Name ______________________ Date __________ Score __________

## Comprehension

**Read the following selection. Then answer questions 1–10 relating to the selection. You may look back at the selection to find the answers.**

Hills of sand up to seven hundred feet high are found in Great Sand Dune National Park. You might think dunes of this size would be near a beach, but they are not. These dunes are in Colorado, far from the ocean. They are the largest in North America. Scientists say that volcanoes once erupted in the area where the San Juan Mountains now stand. Later, as the Sangre de Cristo Mountains were pushed upward, rock under the ash helped form the dunes.

Wind blowing through the area changed the shapes of the dunes. Creeks in the area also played a part. Over the years, five main dune shapes formed.

The most interesting shape for many people is the star. Each of the star's points is formed by winds blowing in a different direction. The tallest dunes are called *reversing dunes.* When most of the winds blow in opposite directions, they make these towering sand deposits.

Winds blowing in only one direction form half-moon shapes. These are called *barchan dunes.* The wind blew straight into them, scooping out the center of these sand mounds and leaving only the outer edges. This can only happen if there is nothing to block the wind's path. The land must be flat and have no plants to stop the movement of the wind. Sometimes rows of these dunes are formed.



GO ON

## Comprehension (continued)

If plants grow in the sand, the wind cannot lift the sand. Instead, the wind blows away the sand around the plants. The dunes left behind are called *parabolic dunes*.

Creeks in the area carry sand that has been blown by the wind from one part of the park to another. So much sand may accumulate in the creeks that it blocks the water's flow. Sand builds up under the water and forms small dams. When enough water backs up, it knocks over the sand dam. This causes surges in the water that look like waves. These creeks are the only ones in the country where waves like this occur.

The dunes are a home for wildlife. Rare insects are found here, too. It is the only place in the world to see the Great Sand Dunes tiger beetle and the giant sand treader camel cricket.

Visitors to the dunes often hike to the top of High Dune. They must follow the ridgelines since there are no trails. Another popular spot is Zapata Falls. This thirty-foot waterfall pours from a crack in the rocks. While there are plenty of sights to see, building a giant sand castle might be the most fun you could have.



GO ON

## Comprehension (continued)

**1.** This story is mostly about

Ⓐ the dams in creeks near sand dunes.

Ⓑ the wildlife that live on sand dunes.

Ⓒ the waterfalls near some sand dunes.

Ⓓ the development of big sand dunes.

**2.** What is most unusual about the Great Sand Dunes?

Ⓐ They have many kinds of wildlife on them.

Ⓑ They are not anywhere near the ocean.

Ⓒ It took a long time for them to be formed.

Ⓓ Their shapes are still changing every day.

**3.** Which of these helped form the Great Sand Dunes initially?

Ⓐ mountains that eroded over a long time

Ⓑ rivers that carried sand away from beaches

Ⓒ water that evaporated and formed sand

Ⓓ rock under ash from volcanoes that erupted

**4.** Which of these does NOT help barchan dunes form?

Ⓐ The wind's path is not blocked by anything.

Ⓑ The wind must blow straight ahead.

Ⓒ The wind scoops out the center of the sand.

Ⓓ The wind blows sand over creeks.

**5.** Parabolic dunes are formed by wind blowing

Ⓐ in a straight line.

Ⓑ in two directions.

Ⓒ around the plants.

Ⓓ up instead of down.

## Comprehension (continued)

**6.** What causes surges in the creek?

Ⓐ lightning hitting the water

Ⓑ water knocking over sand dams

Ⓒ heavy rains that overfill the creek

Ⓓ waterfalls flooding the creek

**7.** How were the dunes shaped and changed?

Ⓐ by the movement of earthquakes

Ⓑ by ancient people digging there

Ⓒ by waterfalls dripping on the sand

Ⓓ by the movement of the wind

**8.** From this selection, you can tell that the dunes

Ⓐ are still being shaped by the winds.

Ⓑ are slowly eroding and getting flat.

Ⓒ are not a good place for plants to grow.

Ⓓ are not a very safe place to visit.

**9.** Why are some rare forms of wildlife found in the dunes?

Ⓐ It is an unusual habitat, so animals adapted to it.

Ⓑ They have been brought here by the wind.

Ⓒ Scientists introduced them here as an experiment.

Ⓓ Zoos have bred new wildlife in this area.

**10.** Why do hikers follow the dune's ridgelines?

Ⓐ They do not want to fall.

Ⓑ The ridgelines take them straight to the top.

Ⓒ There are no trails for hikers to take.

Ⓓ The ridgelines provide more shade.

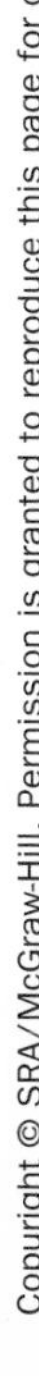


STOP

## Vocabulary

**Read each item. Fill in the bubble for the answer you think is correct.**

1. Rejoin means
   - Ⓐ not join.
   - Ⓑ join again.
   - Ⓒ join many times.
   - Ⓓ want to join.

2. Paid is the base word in prepaid. Prepaid means
   - Ⓐ paid ahead of time.
   - Ⓑ not paid.
   - Ⓒ paid in half.
   - Ⓓ wanting to pay.

3. Dictionary means
   - Ⓐ a group of scientists.
   - Ⓑ a book of number puzzles.
   - Ⓒ a collection of stories.
   - Ⓓ a book of word meanings.

4. What word means about the same as feud?
   - Ⓐ game
   - Ⓑ fight
   - Ⓒ song
   - Ⓓ peace

5. What word means about the same as instruct?
   - Ⓐ forgive
   - Ⓑ convince
   - Ⓒ trick
   - Ⓓ teach

## Vocabulary (continued)

**6.** What word means the opposite of brilliant?

Ⓐ high
Ⓑ dim
Ⓒ bright
Ⓓ hidden

**7.** Which word BEST completes both sentences?

**We should ___ the roof soon.**

**I sewed a ___ on my jacket.**

Ⓐ fix
Ⓑ button
Ⓒ patch
Ⓓ replace

**8.** Which word BEST completes both sentences?

**What will you ___ on the ski trip?**

**The old shoes are showing signs of ___.**

Ⓐ wear
Ⓑ take
Ⓒ see
Ⓓ buy

**9.** Her wisdom was well-known, and the townspeople came to her often for advice.
Wisdom means

Ⓐ ability.
Ⓑ knowledge.
Ⓒ caring.
Ⓓ talent.

**10.** Dad asked our neighbor to help him haul the heavy tree to the truck.
Haul means

Ⓐ chop.
Ⓑ carry.
Ⓒ tie.
Ⓓ glue.

STOP

## Grammar, Usage, and Mechanics

**Read each question. Fill in the bubble beside the answer in each group that is correct. If none of the answers is correct, choose the last answer, "none of the above."**

**1.** Which sentence is written incorrectly?

Ⓐ I learned German from Mrs. Gomez.

Ⓑ Mr. Sanders is the spanish teacher at Brookfield High School.

Ⓒ She graduated from a university in Florida.

Ⓓ none of the above

**2.** Which sentence is written correctly?

Ⓐ Hank hit a double two players crossed home plate.

Ⓑ Hank hit a double; two players crossed home plate.

Ⓒ Hank hit a double, two players crossed home plate.

Ⓓ none of the above

**3.** Which sentence is written correctly?

Ⓐ Lisa said she couldn't never do something like that.

Ⓑ Lisa said she could not never do something like that.

Ⓒ Lisa said she couldn't ever do something like that.

Ⓓ none of the above

**4.** Which sentence is written correctly?

Ⓐ "Our team will take first place, José said.

Ⓑ "Our team will take first place", José said.

Ⓒ Our team will take first place, José said.

Ⓓ none of the above

**5.** Which sentence is written incorrectly?

Ⓐ My dad is older than Frank.

Ⓑ That television show was the most strangest one I have ever seen.

Ⓒ That was the spookiest place I have ever been.

Ⓓ none of the above

GO ON

## Grammar, Usage, and Mechanics (continued)

**6.** Which sentence is written incorrectly?

Ⓐ In summer, lightning often come without rain.

Ⓑ Thunder comes after lightning appears.

Ⓒ Lightning comes often without rain in summer.

Ⓓ none of the above

**7.** Which sentence is written correctly?

Ⓐ Uncle Frank's car is new; our's is old.

Ⓑ Uncle Frank's car is new; our is old.

Ⓒ Uncle Frank's car is new; ours is old.

Ⓓ none of the above

**8.** Which sentence is written correctly?

Ⓐ When Linda hits a home run, the whole team cheers.

Ⓑ When Linda will hit a home run, the whole team cheers.

Ⓒ When Linda hits a home run, the whole team cheered.

Ⓓ none of the above

**9.** Which sentence is written correctly?

Ⓐ Min went to Hollywood to star in a movie.

Ⓑ To be a big movie star in Hollywood.

Ⓒ All the props on the stage in Hollywood.

Ⓓ none of the above

**10.** What type of sentence is this?

**One of the boats in the race had a torn sail and needed repairs.**

Ⓐ Simple

Ⓑ Compound

Ⓒ Complex

Ⓓ Not a sentence

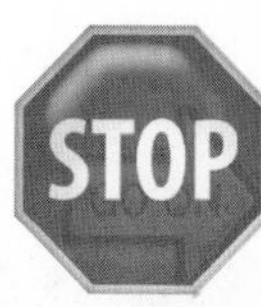

## Spelling

**Read each group of words. Only one of the words is spelled correctly. Fill in the bubble under the word that is spelled correctly.**

| | | | | |
|---|---|---|---|---|
| **1.** | regular | reglar | relugar | regulir |
| | Ⓐ | Ⓑ | Ⓒ | Ⓓ |
| **2.** | chepp | cheap | chaep | chepe |
| | Ⓐ | Ⓑ | Ⓒ | Ⓓ |
| **3.** | suvrey | survay | survey | surviy |
| | Ⓐ | Ⓑ | Ⓒ | Ⓓ |
| **4.** | seam | saem | sem | seemm |
| | Ⓐ | Ⓑ | Ⓒ | Ⓓ |
| **5.** | cieling | ceilin | ceilinng | ceiling |
| | Ⓐ | Ⓑ | Ⓒ | Ⓓ |



GO ON

## Spelling (continued)

**In each sentence, look for the underlined word that is spelled incorrectly. Focus on just the underlined word. Fill in the bubble next to the sentence with the misspelled word. If all the underlined words are spelled correctly, choose "correct as is."**

6. Ⓐ Tina has long, black eylashes.
   Ⓑ Amanda got an award for her piano playing.
   Ⓒ Amy's work is satisfactory.
   Ⓓ correct as is

7. Ⓐ My parents have a lot of knowledge.
   Ⓑ This skysraper is the tallest in the city.
   Ⓒ People who do not take advice are foolish.
   Ⓓ correct as is

8. Ⓐ Ron wrote two papers for extra credit.
   Ⓑ The calves played in the meadow.
   Ⓒ Mom apreciated the flowers we brought her.
   Ⓓ correct as is

9. Ⓐ The knight fought for the king.
   Ⓑ What is the depth of the river here?
   Ⓒ The captain will control the ship.
   Ⓓ correct as is

10. Ⓐ The enemy had to retreat.
    Ⓑ The majorety of the people like the new store.
    Ⓒ Can you extend that ladder to reach the roof?
    Ⓓ correct as is

**This is the end of the group-administered section of the Benchmark Assessment.**

Name ____________________ Date __________ Score __________

# Oral Fluency Assessment

The world's oceans are filled with shipwrecks. Most of 1–9
them lay hidden and forgotten. When one is found, it is a big 10–22
deal. Historians and explorers can study these shipwrecks to 23–31
find out about past cultures. 32–36

One such shipwreck was found in 2003 in the Black Sea. 37–47
The ship sank more than two thousand years ago. This was 48–58
the time when the ancient Greeks lived. Explorers hoped to 59–68
find out more about the Greek civilization from the objects 69–78
they found in the wreck. 79–83

One thing they found in the shipwreck was a pile of huge 84–95
clay jars. The Greeks used these jars to pack and transport 96–106
all kinds of things. The historians wondered what kind of 107–116
things had been carried in these jars. 117–123

The answer to that question became the real "treasure" 124–132
of this shipwreck. When the jars were first studied, fish 133–142
bones were found inside. Fish bones are usually not very 143–152
interesting. But this information was very helpful to the 153–161
explorers and historians. It helped them to understand the 162–170
types of foods ancient Greeks ate. The fish were probably 171–180
going to feed hungry Greek soldiers. 181–186

The oceans are still filled with shipwrecks waiting to be 187–196
found. Some of them hold amazing treasure. Others will give 197–206
information about the lives of people who lived long ago. 207–216

**READING RATE AND ACCURACY**

Total Words Read: ____

Number of Errors: ____

Number of Correct Words Read Per Minute (WPM): ____

Accuracy Rate: ____

(Number of Correct Words Read per Minute ÷ Total Words Read)

**READING FLUENCY**

| | Low | Average | High |
|---|---|---|---|
| Decoding Ability | ○ | ○ | ○ |
| Pace | ○ | ○ | ○ |
| Syntax | ○ | ○ | ○ |
| Self-correction | ○ | ○ | ○ |
| Intonation | ○ | ○ | ○ |

## Oral Fluency Assessment

The world's oceans are filled with shipwrecks. Most of them lay hidden and forgotten. When one is found, it is a big deal. Historians and explorers can study these shipwrecks to find out about past cultures.

One such shipwreck was found in 2003 in the Black Sea. The ship sank more than two thousand years ago. This was the time when the ancient Greeks lived. Explorers hoped to find out more about the Greek civilization from the objects they found in the wreck.

One thing they found in the shipwreck was a pile of huge clay jars. The Greeks used these jars to pack and transport all kinds of things. The historians wondered what kind of things had been carried in these jars.

The answer to that question became the real "treasure" of this shipwreck. When the jars were first studied, fish bones were found inside. Fish bones are usually not very interesting. But this information was very helpful to the explorers and historians. It helped them to understand the types of foods ancient Greeks ate. The fish were probably going to feed hungry Greek soldiers.

The oceans are still filled with shipwrecks waiting to be found. Some of them hold amazing treasure. Others will give information about the lives of people who lived long ago.

Name ______________________ Date __________ Score __________

## Fluency MAZE Assessment

The world's oceans are filled with shipwrecks. Most of them lay hidden and **[yesterday / permission / forgotten]**. When one is found, it is a **[zip / ace / big]** deal. Historians and explorers can study **[wrong / these / blank]** shipwrecks to find out about past **[whether / cultures / accident]**.

One such shipwreck was found in 2003 **[in / of / am]** the Black Sea. The ship sank **[more / can't / dust]** than two thousand years ago. This **[ash / sea / was]** the time when the ancient Greeks **[house / lived / blame]**. Explorers hoped to find out more **[trust / about / quote]** the Greek civilization from the objects **[part / sure / they]** found in the wreck.

One thing **[they / mind / sews]** found in the shipwreck was a **[sing / such / pile]** of huge clay jars. The Greeks **[bowl / used / pass]** these jars to pack and transport **[cot / all / gel]** kinds of things. The historians wondered **[what / band / case]** kind of things had been carried **[ox / in / of]** these jars.

The answer to that **[question / convince / material]** became the real "treasure" of this **[fortunate / conclude / shipwreck]**. When the jars were first studied, **[break / fish / quote]** bones were found inside. Fish bones are **[problem / teacher / usually]** not very interesting. But this information **[era / was / fun]** very helpful to the explorers and **[discrimination / historians / considerations]**. It helped them to understand the **[types / upper / shout]** of foods ancient Greeks ate. The **[sale / thin / fish]** were probably going to feed hungry Greek **[soldiers / backfire / valuable]**.

The oceans are still filled with **[tournament / reputation / shipwrecks]** waiting to be found. Some of **[sill / talk / them]** hold amazing treasure. Others will give **[information / surrender / responsible]** about the lives of people who **[boost / lived / storm]** long ago.

# Expository Writing Prompt

## Directions for Writing

Think about a faraway place that you would like to visit. It can be any place in the world. Write about the place you would like to visit. Describe the place, what it looks like, and what you would do there. Explain why you would like to visit the place.

## Checklist

You will earn the best score if you

- think about the place and plan your writing before you begin.
- make sure your ideas flow in a way that makes sense to your audience.
- provide details so your audience can understand the place.
- use sensory words and descriptive language to describe the place and what you would do.
- avoid words and phrases that are often overused.
- connect the sections of your writing so that nothing seems out of place.
- use correct capital letters, punctuation, and spelling.
- use subjects, verbs, and modifiers correctly.
- write complete sentences and avoid fragments or run-ons.
- read your writing after you finish and check for mistakes.

Name ______________________ Date ________ Score ________

## Comprehension

**Read the following story. Then answer questions 1–10 relating to the story. You may look back at the story to find the answers.**

“Hey, Nate, want to go to the park after school and shoot some baskets?” Allan asked. “Some of the other kids will be there.”

Nate shook his head and responded, “Not today, I have to get home.” Ever since his mom had gone back to work, Nate felt obligated to watch his little sister every afternoon. He did not like it, but he felt he should do it anyway.

An hour later, Nate was reading his favorite book again when Kayla interrupted him for help with her homework. Nate snapped at her to leave him alone. After a few minutes, however, he felt guilty. It was not Kayla’s fault he could not play with his friends.

“What do you need help with, Kayla?” he called. When she brought her math book, he explained how to subtract with regrouping. Kayla seemed surprised at how easy it was and told him he was a great teacher. Nate doubted that, but it made him smile.

That evening at dinner, his mom asked about their day. Kayla told her that Nate had helped her understand borrowing, but Nate just grunted. Later, when Nate and his mother were alone, she asked what was bothering him, and his frustration came pouring out. He told her how he missed playing with his friends after school and how hard it was to take care of Kayla every day.

GO ON

## Comprehension (continued)

His mother looked at him thoughtfully. "I've been so busy worrying about this job, I haven't had a chance to think about how it's affecting you and Kayla. It hasn't been easy for you, but wait a few more months. Once I get settled in this job, I'll be able to make some changes."

The next afternoon, Nate had an idea. Before Kayla's bus arrived, he hurried next door. Mrs. Young took care of them some evenings when their mom had to go shopping. Nate explained that his mom did not have money to pay a babysitter, but he had a plan. Mrs. Young offered to talk to his mom that night.

True to her word, she did. "I know you can't afford to pay for babysitting right now," she said to Nate's mom, "but your son had a fine idea. If I watch Kayla two afternoons a week, Nate has promised to weed my garden every Saturday."

Nate cheered silently when his mom agreed. It would not be easy, but at least he could play with his friends sometimes.



GO ON

## Comprehension (continued)

**1.** This story is mostly about

Ⓐ a boy who helps a neighbor with weeding.

Ⓑ a boy who thinks up a plan to solve a problem.

Ⓒ a boy who helps his sister with homework.

Ⓓ a boy who is frustrated with his sister.

**2.** Nate told Allan he could not play basketball after school because he

Ⓐ was playing video games.

Ⓑ had to weed the yard.

Ⓒ had to watch Kayla.

Ⓓ wanted to do homework.

**3.** Why did Nate watch Kayla after school every day?

Ⓐ He needed the extra money.

Ⓑ Mrs. Young could not babysit her.

Ⓒ Kayla needed help with homework.

Ⓓ He felt it was his responsibility.

**4.** Nate was impatient with Kayla because

Ⓐ he did not want his reading interrupted.

Ⓑ she would not get her homework done.

Ⓒ he had to wait a long time for her bus.

Ⓓ she did not understand her homework.

**5.** Kayla made Nate smile when she said

Ⓐ that she would play basketball with him.

Ⓑ that he was a great teacher.

Ⓒ that she had finished all her homework.

Ⓓ that he was very good at basketball.

## Comprehension (continued)

**6.** What did Nate say was making him frustrated?

Ⓐ having to help Kayla with her homework every day

Ⓑ not doing well when he played basketball

Ⓒ watching Kayla when he wanted to play with friends

Ⓓ not being able to get to the game

**7.** What idea did Nate have to solve his problem?

Ⓐ He closed the door to keep Kayla out.

Ⓑ He asked Mrs. Young to babysit Kayla.

Ⓒ He had Mrs. Young meet Kayla's bus.

Ⓓ He asked his mom for more money.

**8.** In exchange for Mrs. Young's babysitting services

Ⓐ Nate's mom would pay her later.

Ⓑ Kayla would help around the house.

Ⓒ Mom would drive her to the store.

Ⓓ Nate agreed to weed her garden.

**9.** From this story, you can tell that Nate

Ⓐ cares about his younger sister.

Ⓑ is not very good at math homework.

Ⓒ does not have very many friends.

Ⓓ had never worked in a garden before.

**10.** Why does Nate's mom ask him to wait a few more months?

Ⓐ to give her time to change jobs

Ⓑ to give her time to quit her job

Ⓒ to give her time to find a sitter

Ⓓ to give her time to improve the situation

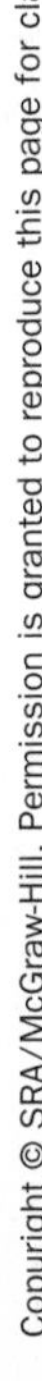


GO ON

Name ______________________ Date __________ Score __________

## Comprehension

**Read the following selection. Then answer questions 1–10 relating to the selection. You may look back at the selection to find the answers.**

When someone makes an invention, they like to patent it. This means they register their idea so people know who thought it up. Over the years, patent offices have seen many weird ideas. Some do make sense. However, no one would want to use them. Others make people wonder if the inventors are serious. During the 1960s and 1970s, Arthur Pedrick came up with some interesting ideas. He had worked in the patent office, so he must have seen many unusual ideas. However, his were some of the strangest.

One of his ideas was a way to get water to the deserts of Africa. This sounded great until people considered his patent. He planned to transfer snowballs from Antarctica through pipelines. He said that Earth's rotation would help pump the snowballs through the tubes. He might have been right. However, no one seemed interested in trying it.

He also wanted to lower air pollution. Again, most people agreed this was important. Because cars are one of the biggest causes of pollution, he came up with a car that did not need fuel. And no one had to buy a new car. They could keep the one they had. All they would have to buy is one of his inventions and a horse.



GO ON

## Comprehension (continued)

He wanted to use a horse to power the car. It may seem like this was going back to the old horse and buggy, but that is not what he had in mind. He planned to put the horse behind the car rather than in front of it. The horse would be hooked up to the car with poles and wires. The horse's feedbox would be close to the car's trunk. When the driver pushed on the gas pedal, the horse's feedbox would move forward. The horse would follow it. As it did, it would push the car forward. The harder the driver pushed on the pedal, the faster the horse (and the car) would go.

The brake pedal was connected to the horse's halter. Pushing on it should bring the horse to a stop. That is, if the driver could push hard enough to stop a speeding or runaway horse. If not, at least the cars would not be going very fast, so accidents would be minor. For some reason, no one wanted to buy this idea either.



GO ON

## Comprehension (continued)

**1.** This story is mostly about

Ⓐ how to get a job in the patent office.

Ⓑ the best way to get inventions patented.

Ⓒ ways to prevent cars from polluting air.

Ⓓ one person's unusual inventions.

**2.** Which of these is NOT a reason why a patent would be useful?

Ⓐ It lets people know who made something.

Ⓑ It will let an inventor keep an idea secret.

Ⓒ It prevents others from stealing an idea.

Ⓓ A patent owner will get paid if the invention is used.

**3.** How did Arthur Pedrick know how to apply for a patent?

Ⓐ His patent lawyer explained it to him.

Ⓑ He had worked in the patent office.

Ⓒ He watched other inventors at work.

Ⓓ He read information about patents.

**4.** Pedrick planned to get water to the deserts by

Ⓐ transferring it from the ocean.

Ⓑ trucking it in barrels.

Ⓒ making irrigation ditches.

Ⓓ sending snowballs through pipelines.

**5.** Pedrick must have known something about science because

Ⓐ he figured the Earth's rotation into one of his inventions.

Ⓑ he liked cars and transportation.

Ⓒ he wanted to lower air pollution.

Ⓓ he applied for patents.

## Comprehension (continued)

**6.** How was Pedrick's car different from a horse and buggy?

Ⓐ The horse pushed instead of pulled the car.

Ⓑ The car pushed the horse instead of pulling it.

Ⓒ The horse could pull the car faster than a buggy.

Ⓓ The car used several horses instead of just one.

**7.** One big disadvantage of Pedrick's car plan is

Ⓐ people who use it must own horses.

Ⓑ it would be hard on the environment.

Ⓒ everyone would need to buy a new car.

Ⓓ most people would speed on highways.

**8.** How did pushing on the gas pedal move the horse?

Ⓐ It gave the horse a shock.

Ⓑ The car pushed the horse ahead.

Ⓒ It moved the feedbox forward.

Ⓓ The pedal turned the wheels.

**9.** From the last paragraph, you can figure out that a horse's halter is something that

Ⓐ protects a horse's feet.

Ⓑ feeds a horse.

Ⓒ causes a horse to stop.

Ⓓ makes a horse stronger.

**10.** From this selection, you can tell that Arthur Pedrick

Ⓐ had no idea how to patent his inventions.

Ⓑ probably had a good sense of humor.

Ⓒ did not know much about Earth's rotation.

Ⓓ was not a very creative person.

STOP

## Vocabulary

**Read each item. Fill in the bubble for the answer you think is correct.**

**1.** Motionless means
- Ⓐ rolling.
- Ⓑ melted.
- Ⓒ still.
- Ⓓ falling.

**2.** Skill is the base word in unskilled. Unskilled means
- Ⓐ without skills.
- Ⓑ highly skilled.
- Ⓒ learning a skill.
- Ⓓ sharing skills.

**3.** Vision means
- Ⓐ the ability to taste.
- Ⓑ the ability to touch.
- Ⓒ the ability to hear.
- Ⓓ the ability to see.

**4.** What word means about the same as delicate?
- Ⓐ pretty
- Ⓑ hardy
- Ⓒ fragile
- Ⓓ damaged

**5.** What word means about the same as proper?
- Ⓐ correct
- Ⓑ heaviest
- Ⓒ expensive
- Ⓓ wrong

## Vocabulary (continued)

**6.** What word means the opposite of victory?

Ⓐ win
Ⓑ tradition
Ⓒ talent
Ⓓ loss

**7.** Which word BEST completes both sentences?

**They will ___ next week.**

**The ___ on this table is beautiful.**

Ⓐ arrive
Ⓑ setting
Ⓒ run
Ⓓ finish

**8.** Which word BEST completes both sentences?

**Doug did not ___ the cold weather.**

**Tell us if you change your ___.**

Ⓐ enjoy
Ⓑ decision
Ⓒ dislike
Ⓓ mind

**9.** The students in the school will attend a special meeting. Attend means

Ⓐ set up.
Ⓑ order.
Ⓒ go to.
Ⓓ enjoy.

**10.** The injured player missed a few games. Injured means

Ⓐ good.
Ⓑ late.
Ⓒ missing.
Ⓓ hurt.

STOP

## Grammar, Usage, and Mechanics

**Read each question. Fill in the bubble beside the answer in each group that is correct. If none of the answers is correct, choose the last answer, "none of the above."**

**1.** Which sentence is written correctly?

Ⓐ Paintings by Degas will be at Penn Art Museum on Tuesday, March 9.

Ⓑ Paintings by Degas will be at Penn Art Museum on tuesday, March 9.

Ⓒ Paintings by Degas will be at Penn art museum on Tuesday, March 9.

Ⓓ none of the above

**2.** Which sentence is written <u>incorrectly</u>?

Ⓐ Five students won gold medals Raul, Lia, Yin, Aaron, and Latoya.

Ⓑ The medals were actually made from these metals: gold, brass, and bronze.

Ⓒ They all had one goal: finish in first place.

Ⓓ none of the above

**3.** Which sentence is written correctly?

Ⓐ Our family never does nothing during vacations.

Ⓑ Our family never does anything during vacations.

Ⓒ Our family doesn't never do anything during vacations.

Ⓓ none of the above

**4.** Which sentence is written correctly?

Ⓐ Pete asked, "Which gift is for Grandma's birthday"?

Ⓑ Pete asked, Which gift is for Grandma's birthday?"

Ⓒ Pete asked, "Which gift is for Grandma's birthday?"

Ⓓ none of the above

**5.** Which sentence is written correctly?

Ⓐ Do you think Mark runs more quickly than Adam?

Ⓑ Do you think Mark runs more quicklier than Adam?

Ⓒ Do you think Mark runs the most quickly than Adam?

Ⓓ none of the above

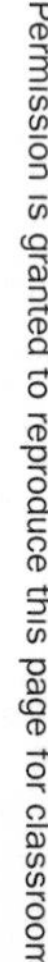


GO ON

## Grammar, Usage, and Mechanics (continued)

**6.** Which sentence is written incorrectly?

Ⓐ The high school and middle school were working on a play.

Ⓑ Julie and Ari loves being on stage in school plays.

Ⓒ In their play, someone always yells from the side.

Ⓓ none of the above

**7.** Which sentence is written correctly?

Ⓐ Maren and him are going to the movies next week.

Ⓑ Maren and his are going to the movies next week.

Ⓒ Him and Maren are going to the movies next week.

Ⓓ none of the above

**8.** Which sentence is written correctly?

Ⓐ When the bell rings, school was over for the day.

Ⓑ When the bell rang, school is over for the day.

Ⓒ When the bell rang, school will be over for the day.

Ⓓ none of the above

**9.** Which sentence is written correctly?

Ⓐ Food for the animals in the zoo.

Ⓑ All the cages of the hungry animals in the Parkline Zoo.

Ⓒ The hungry zebras, tigers, monkeys, and rhinos ate quickly.

Ⓓ none of the above

**10.** What type of sentence is this?

**One hundred large peacocks with their tails fanned out.**

Ⓐ Simple

Ⓑ Compound

Ⓒ Complex

Ⓓ Not a sentence

## Spelling

**Read each group of words. Only one of the words is spelled correctly. Fill in the bubble under the word that is spelled correctly.**

| | | | | |
|---|---|---|---|---|
| **1.** | sefaty | saftey | saffety | safety |
| | Ⓐ | Ⓑ | Ⓒ | Ⓓ |
| **2.** | additional | aditional | aditionnal | additionel |
| | Ⓐ | Ⓑ | Ⓒ | Ⓓ |
| **3.** | presecne | presence | persence | presense |
| | Ⓐ | Ⓑ | Ⓒ | Ⓓ |
| **4.** | farbric | febric | fabrick | fabric |
| | Ⓐ | Ⓑ | Ⓒ | Ⓓ |
| **5.** | fondation | foudation | foundation | fuondasion |
| | Ⓐ | Ⓑ | Ⓒ | Ⓓ |



GO ON

## Spelling (continued)

**In each sentence, look for the underlined word that is spelled incorrectly. Focus on just the underlined word. Fill in the bubble next to the sentence with the misspelled word. If all the underlined words are spelled correctly, choose "correct as is."**

6. Ⓐ The casheir gave us the wrong change.
   Ⓑ Monday is laundry day at our house.
   Ⓒ Sometimes Leah is impatient with her brother.
   Ⓓ correct as is

7. Ⓐ Avery learned a new chord on his guitar.
   Ⓑ The queen chose a jewel for her crown.
   Ⓒ The hikers found pieces of pertrified wood.
   Ⓓ correct as is

8. Ⓐ Liam needed his parents' approval to join.
   Ⓑ My little sister can be a real nuisance!
   Ⓒ Semir's brother is a junour in high school.
   Ⓓ correct as is

9. Ⓐ Pedro likes to plunge right into the water.
   Ⓑ The friends made up after their quarrell.
   Ⓒ The hotel provides breakfast every morning.
   Ⓓ correct as is

10. Ⓐ He gave us an estimate on the house.
    Ⓑ Visitors need a passport to cross the border.
    Ⓒ Do you have something to occupy you while you wait?
    Ⓓ correct as is

**This is the end of the group-administered section of the Benchmark Assessment.**

**Name** ______________________ **Date** __________ **Score** __________

# Oral Fluency Assessment

Flying remote control planes is a hobby that people 1–9
around the world enjoy. In order to learn how to do it, you 10–22
will need a little patience and a good teacher. Most of the 23–34
time, you can find someone who will teach you by checking 35–45
with a flying club. They are all over the country. You also can 46–58
go out to a flying field and ask questions. Veteran flyers are 59–70
more than willing to answer a beginner's questions. 71–78

Find someone who has had many years of flying 79–87
experience. The first few times you go to the field, let your 88–99
instructor control the plane during takeoff and landing. 100–108
Those are the times when the plane is most likely to crash. 109–120
No one learns to fly without a few crashes, so do not feel 121–133
ashamed if it happens. You can reduce the number of crashes 134–144
you have by getting a good instructor. 145–151

Once the plane is in the air, your instructor will hand you 152–163
the controls. When you feel confident that you have the "feel" 164–174
of the controls, you will be ready for your first solo takeoff 175–185
and landing. It will take a lot of practice, but soon you will be 186–199
flying your plane like a pro. Then it will not be long until a 200–213
beginner asks *you* for help! 214–218

**READING RATE AND ACCURACY**

Total Words Read: ____

Number of Errors: ____

Number of Correct Words

Read Per Minute (WPM): ____

Accuracy Rate: ____

(Number of Correct Words Read per Minute ÷ Total Words Read)

**READING FLUENCY**

| | Low | Average | High |
|---|---|---|---|
| Decoding Ability | ○ | ○ | ○ |
| Pace | ○ | ○ | ○ |
| Syntax | ○ | ○ | ○ |
| Self-correction | ○ | ○ | ○ |
| Intonation | ○ | ○ | ○ |

## Oral Fluency Assessment

Flying remote control planes is a hobby that people around the world enjoy. In order to learn how to do it, you will need a little patience and a good teacher. Most of the time, you can find someone who will teach you by checking with a flying club. They are all over the country. You also can go out to a flying field and ask questions. Veteran flyers are more than willing to answer a beginner's questions.

Find someone who has had many years of flying experience. The first few times you go to the field, let your instructor control the plane during takeoff and landing. Those are the times when the plane is most likely to crash. No one learns to fly without a few crashes, so do not feel ashamed if it happens. You can reduce the number of crashes you have by getting a good instructor.

Once the plane is in the air, your instructor will hand you the controls. When you feel confident that you have the "feel" of the controls, you will be ready for your first solo take off and landing. It will take a lot of practice, but soon you will be flying your plane like a pro. Then it will not be long until a beginner asks *you* for help!

## Fluency MAZE Assessment

Flying remote control planes is a hobby that people around the world enjoy. In order to learn how to **[am / my / do]** it, you will need a little patience **[oak / sip / and]** a good instructor. Most of the **[time / just / said]**, you can find someone who will **[might / every / teach]** you by checking with a flying **[both / club / pull]**. They are all over the country. **[You / Eye / Sun]** also can go out to a **[shrink / flying / sooner]** field and ask questions. Veteran flyers **[oil / rob / are]** more than willing to answer a **[themselves / fortunate / beginner's]** questions.

Find someone who has had **[game / self / many]** years of flying experience. The first **[few / nut / add]** times you go to the field, **[rim / let / odd]** your instructor control the plane during **[shovel / natural / takeoff]** and landing. Those are the times **[grab / pour / when]** the plane is most likely to **[crash / group / doubt]**. No one learns to fly without a **[few / rub / cut]** crashes, so do not feel ashamed if **[do / it / my]** happens. You can reduce the number **[so / am / of]** crashes you have by getting a **[good / send / dent]** instructor.

Once the plane is in **[ram / the / mad]** air, your instructor will hand you **[lay / got / the]** controls. After you feel confident that **[air / his / you]** have the "feel" of the controls, **[you / couch / panic]** will be ready for your first **[paper / solo / her]** takeoff and landing. It will take a **[lot / red / who]** of practice, but soon you will be **[grease / flying / league]** your plane like a pro. Then **[we / ox / it]** will not be long until a beginner **[buck / asks / lift]** *you* for help!

Name ______________________ Date __________ Score __________

## Comprehension

**Read the following story. Then answer questions 1–10 relating to the story. You may look back at the story to find the answers.**

"Cranberry picking sure has changed since I was a boy," Grandpa told Cheri as he started the motor of his dry-harvest machine. "Back then, we did everything by hand. Of course, we used the modern metal snap scoop."

He laughed, and Cheri did, too. She had seen the scoop hanging on the wall of the shed, and when she was younger, she had even tried it a few times. Grandpa had saved all the tools his family had used over the years. Mom often teased him that he should start a museum.

A large metal scoop a little over two feet wide was the most modern of the hand tools. The snap scoop was smaller, but it also was made of metal. It had a hinge that snapped open and shut using your thumb. Grandpa's father had bought this special scoop and used it for many years before he could afford the larger scoop.

"Oh, I thought you used that small wooden comb thing," Cheri teased. She knew it had belonged to his grandfather.

Grandpa pretended to be hurt. "I'm not that old. If you don't behave yourself, I'll make you pick berries the way my great grandfather did." He wiggled the fingers of one hand in the air. "Fingers are still the best way."



GO ON

## Comprehension (continued)

"So why don't you use them instead of the machine," she teased him. She already knew the answer. It took hand-pickers a whole day to pick what the machine could harvest in twenty minutes or less.

Grandpa laughed and patted the handle of the machine that looked like a lawnmower and then pushed it forward. Its rotating teeth picked the berries faster than any of his old-fashioned tools could do. Of course, Cheri knew it did not move as fast as wet harvesting machines. Dry harvesting, the kind Grandpa did, was more exacting work. The berries they sold had to be perfect. Wet harvesters moved much faster, since the pickers did not have to worry as much about the berries. If berries got bruised or did not look perfect, it did not matter since they would be made into juice or sauce.

When Grandpa got tired, Cheri ran the machine for a while. She was not as good or as fast as he was, but she was learning. It was hard to keep it going in a straight line, but she managed pretty well. And at the end of the day, as she looked at the day's harvest, Cheri smiled. Sixty-seven barrels of cranberries was not bad for a day's work.



GO ON

## Comprehension (continued)

**1.** This story is mostly about

Ⓐ a grandfather repairing old-fashioned tools.

Ⓑ how to wet harvest cranberries.

Ⓒ a girl picking cranberries with her grandfather.

Ⓓ why dry harvesting is better than wet harvesting.

**2.** What was the earliest tool people used for picking cranberries?

Ⓐ the wooden comb

Ⓑ the metal snap scoop

Ⓒ a harvesting machine

Ⓓ their fingers

**3.** Why do people dry harvest cranberries?

Ⓐ It is easier to do than wet harvesting.

Ⓑ The growing season is much shorter.

Ⓒ It takes much less time to dry harvest.

Ⓓ They need to pick perfect berries to sell whole.

**4.** What is one advantage of wet harvesting cranberries?

Ⓐ Pickers do not worry about berries, so they go fast.

Ⓑ The berries can be harvested much sooner.

Ⓒ Perfect berries are the only ones that are picked.

Ⓓ The berries are wet, so they do not need to be washed.

**5.** Why did Cheri run the dry harvesting machine?

Ⓐ Her parents had bought it for her.

Ⓑ She could run it better than Grandpa.

Ⓒ Her grandfather was feeling tired.

Ⓓ Grandpa could not use modern tools.

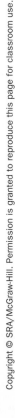

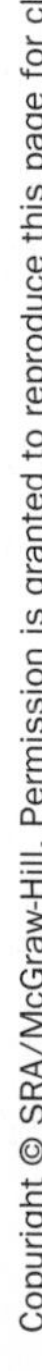


GO ON

## Comprehension (continued)

**6.** What usually happens to wet harvested cranberries?

Ⓐ They are sold whole in bags.

Ⓑ They are crushed for juice or sauce.

Ⓒ They are dried to make new seeds.

Ⓓ They are fed to cattle and pigs.

**7.** Cranberry picking changed over the years in all these ways EXCEPT

Ⓐ motorized machines are used.

Ⓑ most people now use hand tools.

Ⓒ picking has gotten faster.

Ⓓ it has become much easier.

**8.** From this story, you can tell that Cheri

Ⓐ enjoys being with her grandpa.

Ⓑ does not know much about old tools.

Ⓒ has used the harvesting machine many times.

Ⓓ picks cranberries very quickly.

**9.** Which of the following would probably use a wet harvesting machine?

Ⓐ a small farm

Ⓑ an individual berry picker

Ⓒ a company that manufactures cranberry sauce

Ⓓ a company that sells whole berries

**10.** Most pickers do seventy-five barrels a day. Why did Cheri think sixty-seven was good?

Ⓐ She is still learning.

Ⓑ Wet harvesting is slower.

Ⓒ They have a small farm.

Ⓓ They used old tools.

## Comprehension

**Read the following selection. Then answer questions 1–10 relating to the selection. You may look back at the selection to find the answers.**

When the United States became independent from England, Americans wanted a flag for their new nation. Several different versions were used until the first flag law was passed on June 14, 1777. This law said the flag would have red and white stripes and a blue background with stars. At first, the flag had thirteen stars and thirteen stripes. Each stripe stood for one of the thirteen colonies, as did each star.

Because the law did not describe the stars or stripes, most flags looked different. Some stars were in a line, some in a circle. Some flags had six white stripes, but others had seven. Over the years, the flag changed many times. Today there are fifty stars, one for each state, and the stars are sewn in rows onto a blue background. Because the flag is a symbol of the nation, many rules describe how it should be treated.

Flags may be flown any day of the year, but they should be raised for patriotic days and most holidays. There is a special way to raise and lower the flag. The flag should only be raised after sunrise. You should hoist it up the pole quickly. To take it down, lower it slowly anytime before sunset. It is not flown at night unless it is lit up. Only fly the flag in the rain if it is waterproof.

## Comprehension (continued)

Sometimes flags are flown at half-staff. This means the flag flies halfway down the pole. Flags fly at half-staff to show sadness in the country. When a president dies, flags fly at half-staff for thirty days. For vice-presidents or other important officials, it is done for ten days. Sometimes it is also done when there is a national tragedy. The president decides when it should be done.

To fly a flag at half-staff, first raise it all the way to the top of the pole. Hold it there for a second. Then lower it until it is halfway down the pole.

On Memorial Day, the flag is lowered until noon. This reminds people of the sacrifices made for the country. Then the flag is raised to the top of the pole for the rest of the day.

Another rule about the flag is not to hang it with the stars down. Never carry it flat or let it touch the ground. It should fly free. If it is hung with other flags, always put it above or to the right of them. There are even special rules for folding a flag and putting it away.



GO ON

## Comprehension (continued)

**1.** This story is mostly about

Ⓐ the correct way to use and display the American flag.

Ⓑ how the colonies decided on a design for the flag.

Ⓒ why an American flag is lowered to half-staff.

Ⓓ when an American flag is usually flown.

**2.** The first flag law said the American flag would have

Ⓐ stars in a straight line on a dark blue background.

Ⓑ six red stripes and seven white stripes.

Ⓒ stars in a circle above seven red and white stripes.

Ⓓ red and white stripes and stars on a blue background.

**3.** How has the American flag changed over the years?

Ⓐ It has gotten much larger every year.

Ⓑ It now has fifty stars instead of thirteen.

Ⓒ It has a different background color.

Ⓓ It now has seven red and white stripes.

**4.** The main reason people treat the flag with respect is

Ⓐ they see it as a symbol for the country.

Ⓑ they are copying what other people do.

Ⓒ they are impressed by how old the flag is.

Ⓓ they were taught to do it in school.

**5.** How should a flag be raised to the top of a pole?

Ⓐ It should be raised slowly after sunrise.

Ⓑ It should be raised quickly every evening.

Ⓒ It should be raised quickly after sunrise.

Ⓓ It should be raised slowly in the morning.

GO ON

## Comprehension (continued)

**6.** The American flag should be flown

Ⓐ every day in rain or sun.

Ⓑ on the patriotic holidays.

Ⓒ only on Memorial Day.

Ⓓ only over schools and offices.

**7.** The reason the American flag is flown at half-staff is

Ⓐ to get people's attention.

Ⓑ to show great sadness.

Ⓒ to let it fly more freely.

Ⓓ to honor most holidays.

**8.** All of these are rules for using the flag EXCEPT

Ⓐ never carry it flat or let it touch the ground.

Ⓑ do not hang it with the stars down.

Ⓒ only fly waterproof flags in the rain.

Ⓓ fly it at half-staff on weekends.

**9.** From this selection you can tell that the flag

Ⓐ is very important to many Americans.

Ⓑ has not changed much over the years.

Ⓒ is not thought about much.

Ⓓ is rarely flown on American holidays.

**10.** Why would a flag be important to a new country?

Ⓐ to show that it is powerful

Ⓑ to protect it from enemies

Ⓒ to show that it is independent

Ⓓ to explain its struggles

## Vocabulary

**Read each item. Fill in the bubble for the answer you think is correct.**

**1.** Convention means

Ⓐ quarrel.

Ⓑ meeting.

Ⓒ purchase.

Ⓓ surprise.

**2.** Close is the base word in enclose. Enclose means

Ⓐ open widely.

Ⓑ surround.

Ⓒ meet with.

Ⓓ escape from.

**3.** Inspire means

Ⓐ get people to do better.

Ⓑ make people tired.

Ⓒ find new friends.

Ⓓ do something without thinking.

**4.** What word means about the same as peculiar?

Ⓐ strange

Ⓑ pretty

Ⓒ normal

Ⓓ bright

**5.** What word means about the same as frequently?

Ⓐ happily

Ⓑ rarely

Ⓒ plugged

Ⓓ often

## Vocabulary (continued)

6. What word means the opposite of <u>nervous</u>?

Ⓐ calm
Ⓑ tired
Ⓒ anxious
Ⓓ proud

7. What word BEST completes both sentences?

**The ____ was locked at five o'clock.**

**Sandy was ____ at second base.**

Ⓐ safe
Ⓑ door
Ⓒ out
Ⓓ store

8. What word BEST completes both sentences?

**An army ____ is near our town.**

**A large ____ held up the roof.**

Ⓐ post
Ⓑ fort
Ⓒ log
Ⓓ base

9. Jessie was <u>exhausted</u> after running the ten-mile race. <u>Exhausted</u> means

Ⓐ dizzy.
Ⓑ very happy.
Ⓒ very tired.
Ⓓ bruised.

10. The teacher will <u>demonstrate</u> the experiment before the class goes to the lab. <u>Demonstrate</u> means

Ⓐ begin.
Ⓑ show.
Ⓒ fix.
Ⓓ build.

## Grammar, Usage, and Mechanics

**Read each question. Fill in the bubble beside the answer in each group that is correct. If none of the answers is correct, choose the last answer, "none of the above."**

**1.** Which sentence is written correctly?

Ⓐ The yacht *Marlin* won first prize in the Bay city race last Thursday.

Ⓑ The yacht *Marlin* won First prize in the Bay City race last Thursday.

Ⓒ The yacht *Marlin* won first prize in the Bay City race last Thursday.

Ⓓ none of the above

**2.** Which sentence is written correctly?

Ⓐ Trouble comes in threes: I lost my glove, my bat, and my ball.

Ⓑ Trouble comes in threes I lost my glove, my bat, and my ball.

Ⓒ Trouble comes in threes, I lost my glove, my bat, and my ball.

Ⓓ none of the above

**3.** Which sentence is written <u>incorrectly</u>?

Ⓐ I am not leaving these things on the table.

Ⓑ Do not touch none of those things while I am gone.

Ⓒ No one touched anything on my desk.

Ⓓ none of the above

**4.** Which sentence is written correctly?

Ⓐ "wait for me at the corner," Dad told my brother.

Ⓑ "Wait for me at the corner", Dad told my brother.

Ⓒ "Wait for me at the corner," Dad told my brother.

Ⓓ none of the above

**5.** Which sentence is written correctly?

Ⓐ Do you think a pig is more intelligenter than a dog?

Ⓑ Do you think a pig is more intelligent than a dog?

Ⓒ Do you think a pig is most intelligent than a dog?

Ⓓ none of the above

## Grammar, Usage, and Mechanics (continued)

**6.** Which sentence is written correctly?

Ⓐ The cows in the meadow were not eating the grass.

Ⓑ The cows in the meadow was not eating the grass.

Ⓒ In the meadow the cows was not eating the grass.

Ⓓ none of the above

**7.** Which sentence is written correctly?

Ⓐ My friend's costume was scary, but my's was funny.

Ⓑ My friend's costume was scary, but mine's was funny.

Ⓒ My friend's costume was scary, but mine was funny.

Ⓓ none of the above

**8.** Which sentence is written incorrectly?

Ⓐ When the airplane landed, the ground crew began its job.

Ⓑ They opened the hatch and unloaded fifty suitcases.

Ⓒ Part of the crew took the luggage while the rest serviced the plane.

Ⓓ none of the above

**9.** Which sentence is written correctly?

Ⓐ The canoe had to be carried around the rapids.

Ⓑ Rapids that are dangerous and canoes that can tip over.

Ⓒ The most dangerous rapids on the Colorado River.

Ⓓ none of the above

**10.** What type of sentence is this?

**Five workers lifted the heavy beam, and two others nailed it up.**

Ⓐ Simple

Ⓑ Compound

Ⓒ Complex

Ⓓ Not a sentence

## Spelling

**Read each group of words. Only one of the words is spelled correctly. Fill in the bubble under the word that is spelled correctly.**

| | | | | |
|---|---|---|---|---|
| **1.** | eraser | erasur | erraser | eracer |
| | Ⓐ | Ⓑ | Ⓒ | Ⓓ |
| **2.** | wierd | weerd | weird | werid |
| | Ⓐ | Ⓑ | Ⓒ | Ⓓ |
| **3.** | sholarship | scholarship | scholership | scholasrhip |
| | Ⓐ | Ⓑ | Ⓒ | Ⓓ |
| **4.** | fayde | fede | faid | fade |
| | Ⓐ | Ⓑ | Ⓒ | Ⓓ |
| **5.** | terribly | teribly | turibly | terribley |
| | Ⓐ | Ⓑ | Ⓒ | Ⓓ |



GO ON

## Spelling (continued)

**In each sentence, look for the underlined word that is spelled incorrectly. Focus on just the underlined word. Fill in the bubble next to the sentence with the misspelled word. If all the underlined words are spelled correctly, choose "correct as is."**

**6.** Ⓐ How much damage did the accident cause?
Ⓑ Winning the game was a real triumph.
Ⓒ Ellen hunches down before she races.
Ⓓ correct as is

**7.** Ⓐ The cinema has the new movie.
Ⓑ What is the name of the cereal manufactarer?
Ⓒ Peg needed three egg yolks for the cake.
Ⓓ correct as is

**8.** Ⓐ My brother goes to the elementery school.
Ⓑ Please greet the visitors when they arrive.
Ⓒ The recipe said to soften the butter.
Ⓓ correct as is

**9.** Ⓐ The willow tree had long, slender branches.
Ⓑ We always buy school supplies in the summer.
Ⓒ What will you weer to the dance?
Ⓓ correct as is

**10.** Ⓐ My aunt's car is lime green.
Ⓑ The farmer used a tractor to plow.
Ⓒ A helmet will prevent a head injury.
Ⓓ correct as is

**This is the end of the group-administered section of the Benchmark Assessment.**

Name ______________________ Date __________ Score __________

# Oral Fluency Assessment

Alex flopped on the couch and muttered, "But I already 1–10
told Hong I'd take one of her puppies." 11–18

Her mother looked at her sternly and said, "You didn't 19–28
ask me, and you need to be more responsible before you can 29–40
think about having a pet." 41–45

Alex groaned, but her mother continued her lecture. "You 46–54
cannot remember to take out the trash two nights a week, so 55–66
how will you ever remember to feed a dog?" 67–75

"If I prove that I can do it, will you let me get one?" Alex 76–90
asked. 91

Her mother looked thoughtfully at her and answered, "If 92–100
you do all your chores without being reminded for the next 101–111
month, I'll think about it." 112–116

Alex promised she would do all her jobs, and she did. She 117–128
did not complain, and she even kept her room clean. It was a 129–141
lot of work, but she really wanted that puppy. 142–150

On the last day, Alex walked home from school with 151–160
Hong. She would call her mother to ask if she could bring the 161–173
puppy home. But when they arrived, Hong's mother said the 174–183
puppy had gone to a new home that afternoon. Alex hurried 184–194
home so Hong would not see her tears, but when she opened 195–206
her front door, there, to her surprise, was the puppy. 207–216



**READING RATE AND ACCURACY**

Total Words Read: ____

Number of Errors: ____

Number of Correct Words
Read Per Minute (WPM): ____

Accuracy Rate: ____

(Number of Correct Words Read per Minute ÷ Total Words Read)

**READING FLUENCY**

| | Low | Average | High |
|---|---|---|---|
| Decoding Ability | ○ | ○ | ○ |
| Pace | ○ | ○ | ○ |
| Syntax | ○ | ○ | ○ |
| Self-correction | ○ | ○ | ○ |
| Intonation | ○ | ○ | ○ |

## Oral Fluency Assessment

Alex flopped on the couch and muttered, "But I already told Hong I'd take one of her puppies."

Her mother looked at her sternly and said, "You didn't ask me, and you need to be more responsible before you can think about having a pet."

Alex groaned, but her mother continued her lecture. "You cannot remember to take out the trash two nights a week, so how will you ever remember to feed a dog?"

"If I prove that I can do it, will you let me get one?" Alex asked.

Her mother looked thoughtfully at her and answered, "If you do all your chores without being reminded for the next month, I'll think about it."

Alex promised she would do all her jobs, and she did. She did not complain, and she even kept her room clean. It was a lot of work, but she really wanted that puppy.

On the last day, Alex walked home from school with Hong. She would call her mother to ask if she could bring the puppy home. But when they arrived, Hong's mother said the puppy had gone to a new home that afternoon. Alex hurried home so Hong would not see her tears, but when she opened her front door, there, to her surprise, was the puppy.

Name ______________________________ Date __________ Score __________

## Fluency MAZE Assessment

Alex flopped on the couch and muttered, "But I already told Hong I'd take one of her puppies."

Her mother looked at her sternly **[van / die / and]** said, "You didn't ask me, and **[oak / men / you]** need to be more responsible before **[you / pay / her]** can think about having a pet."

Alex **[because / groaned / problem]**, but her mother continued her lecture. "**[You / Sap / Doe]** can't remember to take out the **[tried / trash / ready]** two nights a week, so how **[will / send / does]** you ever remember to feed a **[rub / hoe / dog]**?"

"If I prove that I can **[we / my / do]** it, will you let me get **[can / one / top]**?" Alex asked.

Her mother looked thoughtfully **[at / and / fan]** her and answered, "If you do all your **[second / chores / boring]** without being reminded for the next **[month / young / being]**, I'll think about it."

Alex promised **[twin / last / she]** would do all her jobs, and she **[eat / did / cap]**. She did not complain, and even kept **[mop / kin / her]** room clean. It was a lot **[no / of / me]** work, but she really wanted that **[puppy / erupt / would]**.

On the last day, Alex walked **[buck / home / knew]** from school with Hong. She would call **[ago / her / any]** mother to ask if she could **[issue / sport / bring]** the puppy home. But when they **[experts / arrived / perfect]**, Hong's mother said the puppy had **[gone / tuck / wild]** to a new home that afternoon. Alex **[morning / balance / hurried]** home so Hong would not see her **[under / enjoy / tears]**, but when she opened her front **[door / this / from]**, there, to her surprise, was the **[ready / puppy / thump]**.

Name ______________________ Date __________ Score __________

## Comprehension

**Read the following story. Then answer questions 1–10 relating to the story. You may look back at the story to find the answers.**

Have you ever heard of a "hole in three"?

My dad and I recently flew south for a golf trip. We stayed in a hotel near a beach and drove our rental car to the local golf course. Even if we played poorly, there was always sand and swimming to look forward to when we got back to the hotel. I doubted any of my friends were taking a swim in Atkins Pond while I was swimming in the Atlantic Ocean. They would have had to cut through the ice first.

The "hole in three" happened on the final day of the trip. We were playing a hole with a creek in front of the green, the place where the flag and cup are. I could not hit pretty, high-arcing shots like my father, but I was getting better. I placed my golf ball on a tee and made a few practice swings. I hoped this would be one of my floating shots instead of a dribbler into the creek. I hit the ball and watched it roll slowly into the water.



GO ON

## Comprehension (continued)

I tried it again. The next ball went into the creek, too, but I did not get upset. I was still learning how to play, and Dad said that even the best golfers learn something each time they play. I decided to tee up and hit the ball one more time.

I made two practice swings and stepped up to the ball. It was a solid hit, and the ball flew into the air toward the green. It made it over the creek, landed on the green, bounced once, twice, and rolled by my dad's ball into the cup. I made a hole in one—on the third try!

Dad gave me a hug and said he was proud that I kept trying. The rest of the round was a blur. I hit some other shots that were not that great, but I knew with practice I would get better. After all, I had made a hole in three—a hole in one plus two!



GO ON

## Comprehension (continued)

**1.** This story is mostly about
- Ⓐ the rules of golf.
- Ⓑ a memorable golf shot.
- Ⓒ golf courses in the South.
- Ⓓ how to improve your golf game.

**2.** From what point of view is this story written?
- Ⓐ second-person
- Ⓑ third-person
- Ⓒ first-person
- Ⓓ Dad's point of view

**3.** Why do the narrator and her father fly south?
- Ⓐ to visit family
- Ⓑ to see a ball game
- Ⓒ to fish
- Ⓓ to play golf

**4.** The narrator and her dad stay at a hotel
- Ⓐ on the golf course.
- Ⓑ by the creek.
- Ⓒ near a beach.
- Ⓓ next to a pond.

**5.** How can you tell the story is set during the winter?
- Ⓐ The pond back home is frozen.
- Ⓑ People golf only in the winter.
- Ⓒ The narrator goes to the beach.
- Ⓓ The narrator's dad has a rental car.

## Comprehension (continued)

**6.** Where is the flag on the golf course?

Ⓐ in the creek

Ⓑ on the green

Ⓒ on the tee

Ⓓ in the woods

**7.** The first time the narrator hits the golf ball it goes

Ⓐ onto the green.

Ⓑ into the cup.

Ⓒ into the creek.

Ⓓ over the green.

**8.** How many balls does the narrator hit into the creek?

Ⓐ 1

Ⓑ 5

Ⓒ 3

Ⓓ 2

**9.** According to the story, you know that Dad

Ⓐ got his ball on the green first.

Ⓑ visits the same courses every year.

Ⓒ is impatient on the golf course.

Ⓓ is a professional golfer.

**10.** Based on what you read in the story, the narrator probably

Ⓐ has never played golf before.

Ⓑ has been playing golf for many years.

Ⓒ has no interest in playing golf again.

Ⓓ has been playing golf for a short time.

GO ON

## Comprehension

**Read the following selection. Then answer questions 1–10 relating to the selection. You may look back at the selection to find the answers.**

Long ago, stagecoaches were the best way to travel around the West. Drivers had to be brave and daring. Their routes wove through steep mountain passes. These narrow paths had sharp drops and no rails. Drivers struggled through deep mud and crossed rivers with strong currents. They drove through snow and slid along icy roads. In all kinds of weather, they rode outside of the coach. They had to keep their horses heading in the right path.

Wild animals or a loud noise could startle the horses. If drivers were not strong or careful, their coaches were dragged off by runaway horses. Passengers had to jump out to save their lives. Some coaches blew off the roads during storms. Drivers had to watch for other carts and fallen rocks on the narrow roads. They had to get through, no matter what. Often they carried money, too.

The greatest dangers they faced were outlaws. Robbers lay in wait for them in the mountain passes. Drivers had to be quick to handle the reins. They had to be smart and brave to save themselves and their passengers.



GO ON

## Comprehension (continued)

One driver was shorter and thinner than many of the others. But Charley was known for his bravery. He had never had an accident or been robbed. A shy person, Charley kept to himself a lot. He usually slept with the horses to keep them safe.

Charley was known for the black patch he wore over one of his eyes. He got the patch due to an accident. He had been putting shoes on a horse one day. It kicked him, and he lost an eye.

Charley drove for many years until trains made coaches a thing of the past. Then he retired. When Charley died, people discovered a secret. Charley was a woman. Her real name was Charlotte.

After a newspaper printed her story, many people came forward to tell stories about Charley's bravery. No one knows how many of these stories were true, but Charley became a hero. Everyone wondered how Charley could have fooled people for so many years.

In 1868, Charley even voted for a U.S. president. That might not sound unusual. However, at that time only men could vote. Charley may have been the first woman to vote. No one knows how many other women pretended to be men so they could vote and hold jobs that woman were prevented from doing.



GO ON

## Comprehension (continued)

**1.** This selection is about how

Ⓐ women did not make good stagecoach drivers.

Ⓑ driving a stagecoach was an easy job.

Ⓒ a woman posed as a man and drove a stagecoach.

Ⓓ people voted for president a long time ago.

**2.** Stagecoach drivers had to be brave for all these reasons EXCEPT

Ⓐ they had to drive in all kinds of weather.

Ⓑ they faced robbers and wild animals.

Ⓒ the roads were dangerous and scary.

Ⓓ they often fought with passengers.

**3.** Which of these is NOT a reason why roads were dangerous?

Ⓐ They were winding and steep.

Ⓑ There were no guardrails.

Ⓒ Robbers often lay in wait.

Ⓓ They went into small towns.

**4.** Charley wore a patch because

Ⓐ he liked the way it looked.

Ⓑ he had lost an eye in an accident.

Ⓒ he had an eye infection.

Ⓓ he needed a disguise.

**5.** What happened after trains came to the West?

Ⓐ Stagecoach drivers took different routes.

Ⓑ Stagecoaches were no longer needed.

Ⓒ Stagecoach drivers liked to race trains.

Ⓓ Stagecoaches moved farther north.

## Comprehension (continued)

**6.** Why was it unusual that Charley voted?

Ⓐ Women were not allowed to vote.

Ⓑ Charley did not know how to read.

Ⓒ Men did not often vote back then.

Ⓓ Charley showed no interest in politics.

**7.** What secret did Charley keep all his life?

Ⓐ that he was afraid to drive

Ⓑ that he had lost one eye

Ⓒ that he was a woman

Ⓓ that he had voted

**8.** From this selection, you can tell that

Ⓐ Charley was not a very brave person.

Ⓑ Charley had to learn to drive faster.

Ⓒ Charley did not usually want to vote.

Ⓓ Charley was a very determined person.

**9.** Why did Charlotte have to pretend to be someone else?

Ⓐ to have a job women were not allowed to do

Ⓑ to keep safe from robbers on the roads

Ⓒ to hide out from the law

Ⓓ to avoid people from her past

**10.** Why do you think Charley kept to himself?

Ⓐ He did not want people to know his secret.

Ⓑ He was shy around other people.

Ⓒ He was embarrassed about the way his eye looked.

Ⓓ He preferred the company of horses to people.

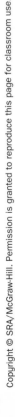

## Vocabulary

**Read each item. Fill in the bubble for the answer you think is correct.**

1. Independence means
   - Ⓐ requirement.
   - Ⓑ peaceful.
   - Ⓒ confusion.
   - Ⓓ freedom.

2. Serve is the base word in servant. Servant means
   - Ⓐ the way that something is served.
   - Ⓑ plates on which food is served.
   - Ⓒ someone who serves.
   - Ⓓ food that is served.

3. Nautical means
   - Ⓐ about clouds and rain.
   - Ⓑ relating to the ocean.
   - Ⓒ dealing with rocks.
   - Ⓓ involved with outer space.

4. What word means about the same as grumpy?
   - Ⓐ sick
   - Ⓑ happy
   - Ⓒ crabby
   - Ⓓ late

5. What word means about the same as concerned?
   - Ⓐ carefree
   - Ⓑ lazy
   - Ⓒ worried
   - Ⓓ quick

## Vocabulary (continued)

**6.** What word means the opposite of ordinary?

Ⓐ typical
Ⓑ free
Ⓒ unusual
Ⓓ natural

**7.** Which word BEST completes both sentences?

**You can earn ___ on your money.**

**Her greatest ___ is African art.**

Ⓐ profits
Ⓑ enjoyment
Ⓒ payment
Ⓓ interest

**8.** Which word BEST completes both sentences?

**The ___ is closed for the holiday.**

**The ___ of the stream is muddy.**

Ⓐ bank
Ⓑ store
Ⓒ side
Ⓓ park

**9.** The compact car could not hold five passengers.
Compact means

Ⓐ foreign.
Ⓑ broken.
Ⓒ old.
Ⓓ small.

**10.** The secretive artist will not reveal her new painting before the show opens.
Reveal means

Ⓐ uncover.
Ⓑ sell.
Ⓒ draw.
Ⓓ take.

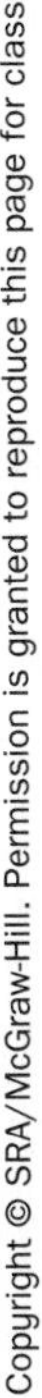


STOP

## Grammar, Usage, and Mechanics

**Read each question. Fill in the bubble beside the answer in each group that is correct. If none of the answers is correct, choose the last answer, "none of the above."**

**1.** Which sentence is written incorrectly?

Ⓐ The Empire State Building is in New York City.

Ⓑ We took a vacation to six European Countries.

Ⓒ I have seen San Francisco's Golden Gate Bridge.

Ⓓ none of the above

**2.** Which sentence is written correctly?

Ⓐ Monkeys will eat bananas, some also like to eat peanuts.

Ⓑ Monkeys will eat bananas some also like to eat peanuts.

Ⓒ Monkeys will eat bananas; some also like to eat peanuts.

Ⓓ none of the above

**3.** Which sentence is written correctly?

Ⓐ Leng's father hardly ever visits his family in Vietnam.

Ⓑ Leng's father hardly never visits his family in Vietnam.

Ⓒ Leng's father does not hardly never visit his family in Vietnam.

Ⓓ none of the above

**4.** Which sentence is written correctly?

Ⓐ "this is the stage door," the dance teacher said.

Ⓑ "This is the stage door", the dance teacher said.

Ⓒ "This is the stage door," The dance teacher said.

Ⓓ none of the above

**5.** Which sentence is written correctly?

Ⓐ My dad thinks Smith is the greatest boxer of all time.

Ⓑ My dad thinks Smith is the most greatest boxer of all time.

Ⓒ My dad thinks Smith is the greater boxer of all time.

Ⓓ none of the above

## Grammar, Usage, and Mechanics (continued)

**6.** Which sentence is written incorrectly?

Ⓐ Jungle animals find food in rivers and on land.

Ⓑ Some get their food by swimming.

Ⓒ The tiger in the jungle stalk its prey.

Ⓓ none of the above

**7.** Which sentence is written correctly?

Ⓐ Ron threw the ball to Pam; he thought she would catch them.

Ⓑ Ron threw the ball to Pam; he thought she would catch it.

Ⓒ Ron threw the ball to Pam; he thought her would catch it.

Ⓓ none of the above

**8.** Which sentence is written correctly?

Ⓐ The coach was teaching us a new play, so we will all listen closely.

Ⓑ The coach taught us a new play, so we all listened closely.

Ⓒ The coach will teach us a new play, so we all listened closely.

Ⓓ none of the above

**9.** Which sentence is written correctly?

Ⓐ When it rains, the mountain streams overflow.

Ⓑ Mountain streams, waterfalls, and flowing rivers.

Ⓒ Rains stopped but streams keep running and moving.

Ⓓ none of the above

**10.** What type of sentence is this?

**When summer comes, Anna enjoys swimming in the pool.**

Ⓐ Simple

Ⓑ Compound

Ⓒ Complex

Ⓓ Not a sentence

STOP

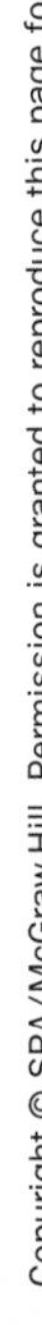

## Spelling

**Read each group of words. Only one of the words is spelled correctly. Fill in the bubble under the word that is spelled correctly.**

| | | | | |
|---|---|---|---|---|
| **1.** | exmpt | exemtp | exemept | exempt |
| | Ⓐ | Ⓑ | Ⓒ | Ⓓ |
| **2.** | fiathful | faithful | faithfull | faythful |
| | Ⓐ | Ⓑ | Ⓒ | Ⓓ |
| **3.** | refewge | reffugy | refuge | refug |
| | Ⓐ | Ⓑ | Ⓒ | Ⓓ |
| **4.** | unbeaten | unbaeten | unebaten | unbeatten |
| | Ⓐ | Ⓑ | Ⓒ | Ⓓ |
| **5.** | wedth | widht | wiedth | width |
| | Ⓐ | Ⓑ | Ⓒ | Ⓓ |



GO ON

## Spelling (continued)

**In each sentence, look for the underlined word that is spelled incorrectly. Focus on just the underlined word. Fill in the bubble next to the sentence with the misspelled word. If all the underlined words are spelled correctly, choose "correct as is."**

**6.** Ⓐ Lily's directions were misleading.
Ⓑ No one knew what the object was.
Ⓒ My dog will bury any bone he finds.
Ⓓ correct as is

**7.** Ⓐ Use arrows to indicate the correct path.
Ⓑ Tim packed a suitcase for the trip.
Ⓒ That light swich does not work.
Ⓓ correct as is

**8.** Ⓐ Lora had a file for her favorite pictures.
Ⓑ Henri was the only pasenger on the train.
Ⓒ In late afternoon, the tree casts a long shadow.
Ⓓ correct as is

**9.** Ⓐ Most stories have at least one herioic figure.
Ⓑ Strong winds caused the snow to drift.
Ⓒ Visitors are limited to this side of the castle.
Ⓓ correct as is

**10.** Ⓐ Can we come to an agreement?
Ⓑ Our class is taking a field trip to the musuem.
Ⓒ Some animals are bred for strength.
Ⓓ correct as is

**This is the end of the group-administered section of the Benchmark Assessment.**

Name ______________________ Date __________ Score __________

# Oral Fluency Assessment

Crop circles first made the news in the 1980s. Few people 1–11
had heard of crop circles before then, but then the first 12–22
circles were discovered in England. These circles of crushed 23–31
plants appeared in the middle of fields. If humans made the 32–42
circles, they left no clues. How could they have gotten into 43–53
the field without leaving any traces? 54–59

Right away, some people thought of aliens, believing 60–67
that spaceships might have left the marks. Other people 68–76
thought the weather or natural forces made them. Scientists 77–85
wondered if strong winds or changes in the soil caused the 86–96
marks. 97

For years, people were not really sure. Then in 1991, two 98–108
men claimed they made the circles. They sneaked into the 109–118
fields at night by walking between rows of crops. Using 119–128
string and a board, they flattened the grass into a circle. 129–139
They each wore a cap with a loop of wire over one eye. 140–152
Looking through the loop at a landmark helped them keep 153–162
the circles straight. 163–165

Although the men said they had made circles, they had 166–175
not made all of them. Crop circles have been found in many 176–187
countries. Others may have copied their idea, but some 188–196
people still wonder if humans have made all crop circles. 197–206

**READING RATE AND ACCURACY**

Total Words Read: ____

Number of Errors: ____

Number of Correct Words Read Per Minute (WPM): ____

Accuracy Rate: ____

(Number of Correct Words Read per Minute ÷ Total Words Read)

**READING FLUENCY**

| | Low | Average | High |
|---|---|---|---|
| Decoding Ability | ○ | ○ | ○ |
| Pace | ○ | ○ | ○ |
| Syntax | ○ | ○ | ○ |
| Self-correction | ○ | ○ | ○ |
| Intonation | ○ | ○ | ○ |

## Oral Fluency Assessment

Crop circles first made the news in the 1980s. Few people had heard of crop circles before then, but then the first circles were discovered in England. These circles of crushed plants appeared in the middle of fields. If humans made the circles, they left no clues. How could they have gotten into the field without leaving any traces?

Right away, some people thought of aliens, believing that spaceships might have left the marks. Other people thought the weather or natural forces made them. Scientists wondered if strong winds or changes in the soil caused the marks.

For years, people were not really sure. Then in 1991, two men claimed they made the circles. They sneaked into the fields at night by walking between rows of crops. Using string and a board, they flattened the grass into a circle. They each wore a cap with a loop of wire over one eye. Looking through the loop at a landmark helped them keep the circles straight.

Although the men said they had made circles, they had not made all of them. Crop circles have been found in many countries. Others may have copied their idea, but some people still wonder if humans have made all crop circles.

Name ______________________ Date __________ Score __________

## Fluency MAZE Assessment

Crop circles first made the news in the 1980s. Few people had heard of crop **[problem / circles / incline]** before then, but then the first **[dreamed / thought / circles]** were discovered in England. These circles **[so / of / it]** crushed plants appeared in the middle **[of / by / no]** fields. If humans made the circles, **[hard / says / they]** left no clues. How could they **[have / fame / care]** gotten into the field without leaving **[any / sit / are]** traces?

Right away, some people thought **[we / of / so]** aliens, believing that spaceships might have **[left / sink / idea]** the marks. Other people thought the **[recently / improve / weather]** or natural forces made them. Scientists **[wondered / footstep / daughter]** if strong winds or changes in **[out / the / ask]** soil caused the marks.

For **[homes / years / novel]**, people were not really sure. Then in 1991, **[two / are / led]** men claimed they made the circles. **[Heat / Show / They]** sneaked into the fields at night **[so / by / us]** walking between rows of crops. Using **[easier / string / should]** and a board, they flattened the **[grass / makes / songs]** into a circle. They each wore a **[cap / sip / law]** with a loop of wire over **[rip / toe / one]** eye. Looking through the loop at a **[landmark / convince / reassure]** helped them keep the circles straight.

**[Splendid / Although / Reviewed]** the men said they had made **[morning / circles / playing]**, they had not made all of them. **[Ever / Rock / Crop]** circles have been found in many **[guideline / something / countries]**. Others may have copied their idea, **[but / he's / own]** some people still wonder if humans **[colt / sons / have]** made all crop circles.

# Expository Writing Prompt

## Writing Situation

Think about an interesting person in your family. Write about the person. Describe what the person looks like, tell where the person lives, and explain how the person is related to you. Explain why you find this person so interesting.

## Checklist

You will earn the best score if you

- think about the person and plan your writing before you begin.
- make sure your ideas flow in a way that makes sense to your audience.
- provide sufficient details about the person.
- use sensory words and descriptive language to describe the person and what makes him or her interesting.
- avoid words and phrases that are often overused.
- connect the sections of your writing so that nothing seems out of place.
- use correct capital letters, punctuation, and spelling.
- use subjects, verbs, and modifiers correctly.
- write complete sentences and avoid fragments or run-ons.
- read your writing after you finish and check for mistakes.

Name ________________________ Date __________ Score __________

## Comprehension

**Read the following story. Then answer questions 1–10 relating to the story. You may look back at the story to find the answers.**

As he watched out the window, Lee saw his friends practicing their moves. They were boarding in a skateboard park that the city had built across the street. Tyree zipped down a halfpipe and crouched low. With his board tilted, he rose over the edge a few feet, turned in midair, and descended. Several of his friends followed, and even Tamika, who had just started, was practicing difficult moves. She jumped, and while in the air, spun her board around once.

Lee sighed deeply. He wished he could join them. If he went over, his friends would let him use a skateboard for a while, but then he would have to give it back. He could not practice for hours on the weekends like they did. Lee wanted a board of his own, but he did not have enough money.

The next afternoon, Lee walked to the sporting goods store a few blocks away and stared through the window. A girl he knew boarded past, did a full turn, and headed back. "There's a place on Sixth Street that sells used boards," she said. "They're a lot cheaper than this."

A few minutes later, Lee went to the store. The girl was right; the store had good prices. Some of the skateboards were not in great condition. He did find two, however, that were decent.

GO ON

## Comprehension (continued)

When a salesperson asked if he could help, Lee mumbled, "I like this board, but can't afford it."

"If you have any used sports equipment, we take trades," the man said.

Lee's eyes lit up and he asked, "Would you take baseball stuff?"

When the man said they would, Lee hurried home. He dug out his old bat, ball, and glove from the chest in his room. He sorted through the storage cage in the basement of the apartment building for things his older brother had left behind. His mom added her old tennis racket and a pair of skis to the pile.

The next day, Tyree helped Lee carry everything to the Sixth Street store. Then Tyree checked out the skateboard Lee planned to buy while the salesperson looked over the trades. "This skateboard has rubber wheels, which are the fastest," Tyree said. "I'd get this one."

The man added up everything and said it would cost Lee five dollars after his trades. Lee only had two dollars, but Tyree dug through his pockets and pulled out several dollars himself. Although Lee protested, Tyree insisted on paying, so Lee promised to repay him as soon as possible.

"No hurry," Tyree replied. "I'm just glad my best friend can skateboard with me at last."



GO ON

## Comprehension (continued)

**1.** This story is mostly about

Ⓐ a boy who wants a skateboard.

Ⓑ how to choose a new skateboard.

Ⓒ a girl who helps with a problem.

Ⓓ how to do new skateboard moves.

**2.** What were Lee's friends doing while he watched?

Ⓐ They were going to skateboarding competitions.

Ⓑ They were checking out prices of skateboards.

Ⓒ They were playing basketball at the park.

Ⓓ They were practicing their skateboarding moves.

**3.** In the beginning, why did Lee not have a skateboard?

Ⓐ His mom thought they were dangerous.

Ⓑ He did not know how to ride one.

Ⓒ He could not afford one.

Ⓓ His friends would not let him borrow theirs.

**4.** Who told Lee about another place to shop?

Ⓐ a girl who was skateboarding past

Ⓑ the store owner with the new skateboards

Ⓒ his mother, who had heard about it

Ⓓ Lee's friends who were skateboarding

**5.** What did Lee do to pay for his skateboard?

Ⓐ borrowed money from his friends

Ⓑ asked his mother for money to pay for it

Ⓒ traded used sports equipment for it

Ⓓ worked hard after school to make money

## Comprehension (continued)

6. Lee brings all of the following to the Sixth Street store EXCEPT
   Ⓐ his mother's skies.
   Ⓑ his aunt's football.
   Ⓒ things his brother had left behind.
   Ⓓ his old baseball equipment.

7. From this story, you can tell that
   Ⓐ Lee's mom worries about him skateboarding.
   Ⓑ Tamika knows a lot about skateboarding.
   Ⓒ Lee will not do well at skateboarding.
   Ⓓ Tyree is a helpful and caring friend.

8. What did Tyree say would make the skateboard fast?
   Ⓐ greasing the wheels
   Ⓑ its rubber wheels
   Ⓒ the rounded ends
   Ⓓ new metal wheels

9. How did Tyree help Lee out at the end?
   Ⓐ Tyree gave Lee three dollars.
   Ⓑ Tyree showed Lee new moves.
   Ⓒ Tyree helped Lee fix a wheel.
   Ⓓ Tyree went to the park with Lee.

10. How can you tell that skateboarding is popular where Lee lives?
   Ⓐ Lee's friends spend time practicing their moves.
   Ⓑ Skateboards are sold at sporting goods stores.
   Ⓒ The city built a park just for skateboarders.
   Ⓓ People can trade items for skateboards.

## Comprehension

**Read the following selection. Then answer questions 1–10 relating to the selection. You may look back at the selection to find the answers.**

The world knows Albert Einstein as one of the smartest people in history. His theories about space and time shape how we think about the world. Even his name is used to describe a smart person—an "Einstein." Who would have thought that such an intelligent person would drop out of school because his teachers did not think he was smart?

Einstein was born in Germany in 1879. Like most children at the time, he started school when he was six years old. For an odd reason, there was trouble from the start.

Einstein was a thoughtful boy who did not like to give quick answers. He also learned that his teachers were not pleased with students who gave wrong answers. His solution made sense to him but not to his teachers. What he did was think about his answers for a long time before he spoke out loud. Answering slowly made some teachers think that he was not smart.

It did not help matters that Einstein would not study subjects that bored him. He liked math, so he got good grades in that subject. But he did not do the rest of his work. He got poor grades in almost everything else. Many people did not know what to make of him.



GO ON

## Comprehension (continued)

By the time Einstein was fifteen years old, things had gotten worse at school and at home. He did not like sports, so the other students thought he was weird. He had very few friends. His father's business was failing.

The family received an offer to move to Italy. There was a big problem, however, at least from Albert's point of view. He still had one year of school left. The rest of the family agreed that he should stay behind in Germany and finish school.

By now Einstein hated school. He had no friends, and his teachers disliked him. They thought he was not trying. Finally, Einstein begged his family to allow him to leave school. They saw how sad he was, so they said he could. At the age of fifteen, Albert Einstein became a high-school dropout.

The young Einstein eventually finished school. It would not be long before he changed physics with his ideas and became the most famous scientist in the world. Years later, he would chuckle that his teachers once thought he could not learn.



GO ON

## Comprehension (continued)

**1.** This selection is mostly about

Ⓐ how Einstein changed physics.

Ⓑ what school was like in Germany.

Ⓒ Einstein's struggles in school.

Ⓓ becoming a famous scientist.

**2.** What did Einstein develop that changed the world's thinking?

Ⓐ theories about space and time

Ⓑ ideas on how to get to the moon

Ⓒ ways to make engines more efficient

Ⓓ new approaches to art and science

**3.** Today, a student might be called an "Einstein" if he or she

Ⓐ does very poorly in school.

Ⓑ does not turn in homework.

Ⓒ is extremely intelligent.

Ⓓ gives teachers trouble.

**4.** Einstein's teachers believed he was

Ⓐ not very smart.

Ⓑ a brilliant student.

Ⓒ a hard worker.

Ⓓ always in trouble.

**5.** All of these were problems for Einstein in school EXCEPT

Ⓐ he did not like to give quick answers.

Ⓑ his teachers did not understand him.

Ⓒ he only did work when he was interested in it.

Ⓓ he was not very smart, so he did poorly.

## Comprehension (continued)

**6.** At age fifteen, all of these were problems for Einstein EXCEPT

Ⓐ other students thought he was weird.

Ⓑ his father's business was failing.

Ⓒ his teachers thought little of him.

Ⓓ having to travel to the United States.

**7.** When his family moved to Italy, Einstein

Ⓐ dropped out of high school.

Ⓑ stayed in Germany and finished high school.

Ⓒ switched to a school in Italy.

Ⓓ graduated from an Italian college.

**8.** What might have helped Einstein do better in school?

Ⓐ having teachers who were stricter

Ⓑ having schoolwork that interested him

Ⓒ having someone help him with his homework

Ⓓ having more subjects to study

**9.** After Einstein became famous, he was amused that

Ⓐ he was not smart, but he had done well in school.

Ⓑ his teachers always thought he could not learn.

Ⓒ all the other students had thought he was weird.

Ⓓ he had never remembered to do his homework.

**10.** One thing this selection shows you is that

Ⓐ moving to another country helps solve problems.

Ⓑ students who do poorly can be successful later.

Ⓒ teachers like students who give wrong answers.

Ⓓ scientists have problems with schoolwork.

STOP

## Vocabulary

**Read each item. Fill in the bubble for the answer you think is correct.**

1. Predict means
   Ⓐ make things from long ago.
   Ⓑ solve a problem.
   Ⓒ write about people.
   Ⓓ tell about the future.

2. Admire is the base word in admiration. Admiration means
   Ⓐ respect.
   Ⓑ fear.
   Ⓒ explanation.
   Ⓓ improvement.

3. Spectator means
   Ⓐ a type of clock.
   Ⓑ someone who watches.
   Ⓒ large piles of sand.
   Ⓓ strong winds.

4. What word means about the same as phase?
   Ⓐ speech
   Ⓑ trip
   Ⓒ completion
   Ⓓ stage

5. What word means about the same as delay?
   Ⓐ play
   Ⓑ wait
   Ⓒ start
   Ⓓ turn

## Comprehension (continued)

**6.** What word means the opposite of clumsy?

Ⓐ awkward
Ⓑ tall
Ⓒ graceful
Ⓓ hungry

**7.** Which word BEST completes both sentences?

**This ___ shows the cost of each car.**

**Our ___ has wooden legs.**

Ⓐ table
Ⓑ counter
Ⓒ tag
Ⓓ desk

**8.** Which word BEST completes both sentences?

**The ___ had a good game.**

**Pour the orange juice from the ___.**

Ⓐ player
Ⓑ pitcher
Ⓒ bottle
Ⓓ team

**9.** The judge said she was innocent, so she was free to go. Innocent means.

Ⓐ young.
Ⓑ understanding.
Ⓒ neglected.
Ⓓ blameless.

**10.** The cows graze on the tasty grass in the field. Graze means

Ⓐ feed.
Ⓑ sleep.
Ⓒ run.
Ⓓ lie.

STOP

## Grammar, Usage, and Mechanics

**Read each question. Fill in the bubble beside the answer in each group that is correct. If none of the answers is correct, choose the last answer, "none of the above."**

1. Which sentence is written correctly?
   - Ⓐ His ancestors fought at gettysburg during the Civil War.
   - Ⓑ His Ancestors fought at Gettysburg during the civil war.
   - Ⓒ His ancestors fought at Gettysburg during the Civil War.
   - Ⓓ none of the above

2. Which sentence is written incorrectly?
   - Ⓐ Do not touch that red switch it's dangerous!
   - Ⓑ A friend touched the switch; he burned his finger.
   - Ⓒ There is one rule to follow: Leave the red switch alone!
   - Ⓓ none of the above

3. Which sentence is written incorrectly?
   - Ⓐ She did not see anything new.
   - Ⓑ I never miss any games.
   - Ⓒ Our team hardly never wins no games.
   - Ⓓ none of the above

4. Which sentence is written correctly?
   - Ⓐ "The director asked," Who will be at the concert?
   - Ⓑ The director asked, Who will be at the concert?
   - Ⓒ The director asked, "Who will be at the concert?"
   - Ⓓ none of the above

5. Which sentence is written correctly?
   - Ⓐ The drummer played the loudest of all the parade marchers.
   - Ⓑ The drummer played the most loudest of all the parade marchers.
   - Ⓒ The drummer played the most louder of all the parade marchers.
   - Ⓓ none of the above

## Grammar, Usage, and Mechanics (continued)

**6.** Which sentence is written correctly?

Ⓐ I wants to be an astronaut like you.

Ⓑ The girl with the braids runs fast.

Ⓒ The smallest bird in the trees were chirping.

Ⓓ none of the above

**7.** Which sentence is written correctly?

Ⓐ She and him both wanted to walk to his store.

Ⓑ She and he both wanted to walk to his store.

Ⓒ Her and he both wanted walk to him store.

Ⓓ none of the above

**8.** Which sentence is written correctly?

Ⓐ The lion chased the zebra through the grass, but the zebra will get away.

Ⓑ The lion chases the zebra through the grass, but the zebra got away.

Ⓒ The lion will chase the zebra through the grass, but the zebra gets away.

Ⓓ none of the above

**9.** Which sentence is written correctly?

Ⓐ Paul helped the engineer make the machine work.

Ⓑ The machine with its many different cogs and wheels.

Ⓒ Paul's knowledge of machines and engines.

Ⓓ none of the above

**10.** What type of sentence is this?

**As the Iron Age progressed, humans invented new tools.**

Ⓐ Simple

Ⓑ Compound

Ⓒ Complex

Ⓓ Not a sentence

STOP

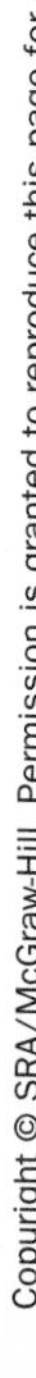

## Spelling

**Read each group of words. Only one of the words is spelled correctly. Fill in the bubble under the word that is spelled correctly.**

| | | | | |
|---|---|---|---|---|
| **1.** | frouth | forth | ferth | forht |
| | Ⓐ | Ⓑ | Ⓒ | Ⓓ |
| **2.** | miosture | moystur | moisture | misture |
| | Ⓐ | Ⓑ | Ⓒ | Ⓓ |
| **3.** | district | distrect | districk | distict |
| | Ⓐ | Ⓑ | Ⓒ | Ⓓ |
| **4.** | opinar | openur | oponer | opener |
| | Ⓐ | Ⓑ | Ⓒ | Ⓓ |
| **5.** | corts | courts | courst | curts |
| | Ⓐ | Ⓑ | Ⓒ | Ⓓ |



GO ON

## Spelling (continued)

**In each sentence, look for the underlined word that is spelled incorrectly. Focus on just the underlined word. Fill in the bubble next to the sentence with the misspelled word. If all the underlined words are spelled correctly, choose "correct as is."**

**6.** Ⓐ The cowboy removed his horse's saddle.
Ⓑ Please glue these stars on that poster.
Ⓒ What is the diameter of a circle?
Ⓓ correct as is

**7.** Ⓐ The mayer gave a speech.
Ⓑ Our team was excited when we won.
Ⓒ Dad deposited a check in the bank.
Ⓓ correct as is

**8.** Ⓐ The ending of the movie was abrupt.
Ⓑ My dad is worried about the expanding town.
Ⓒ The river was too braod to wade across it.
Ⓓ correct as is

**9.** Ⓐ The ship dropped ancher in the harbor.
Ⓑ Does this make sense now?
Ⓒ He felt no hatred for the team.
Ⓓ correct as is

**10.** Ⓐ Joan writes in her journal once a week.
Ⓑ The children in the preschool are behaveing well.
Ⓒ Show respect for your parents!
Ⓓ correct as is

**This is the end of the group-administered section of the Benchmark Assessment.**

Name ______________________ Date __________ Score __________

## Oral Fluency Assessment

Kelly had been eagerly awaiting her favorite time of year. 1–10
She checked the temperature every day until at last, during 11–20
the final week of March, the weather was warm enough. 21–30
The family members put on warm clothes, gathered their 31–39
supplies, and trekked into the woods. 40–45

"Here's a tree that's big enough, Dad," Kelly called. 46–54

Everyone hurried over to join her. They checked the tree 55–64
for old scars, and then Dad drilled three holes in the bark and 65–77
tapped in spouts. Kelly and her mom hung buckets on the 78–88
spouts and covered them. Now all they had to do was wait 89–100
for the buckets to fill with sap. 101–107

When the buckets were full, they collected them and 108–116
carried them back to the house. Dad lit the fire in the outdoor 117–129
fireplace. They did not make syrup in the kitchen because 130–139
boiling sap made too much steam. Dad rubbed a little oil 140–150
around the rim of the pot to help keep the sap from bubbling 151–163
over. Then he poured some sap into the pot, and as the sap 164–176
boiled down, he added more. 177–181

Once it was done, they poured it into clean bottles. It was 182–193
a lot of work for such a little bit of syrup, but they thought 194–207
the effort was worth it, at least Kelly thought so. 208–217

**READING RATE AND ACCURACY**

Total Words Read: ____

Number of Errors: ____

Number of Correct Words Read Per Minute (WPM): ____

Accuracy Rate: ____

(Number of Correct Words Read per Minute ÷ Total Words Read)

**READING FLUENCY**

| | Low | Average | High |
|---|---|---|---|
| Decoding Ability | ○ | ○ | ○ |
| Pace | ○ | ○ | ○ |
| Syntax | ○ | ○ | ○ |
| Self-correction | ○ | ○ | ○ |
| Intonation | ○ | ○ | ○ |

## Oral Fluency Assessment

Kelly had been eagerly awaiting her favorite time of year. She checked the temperature every day until at last, during the final week of March, the weather was warm enough. The family members put on warm clothes, gathered their supplies, and trekked into the woods.

"Here's a tree that's big enough, Dad," Kelly called.

Everyone hurried over to join her. They checked the tree for old scars, and then Dad drilled three holes in the bark and tapped in spouts. Kelly and her mom hung buckets on the spouts and covered them. Now all they had to do was wait for the buckets to fill with sap.

When the buckets were full, they collected them and carried them back to the house. Dad lit the fire in the outdoor fireplace. They did not make syrup in the kitchen because boiling sap made too much steam. Dad rubbed a little oil around the rim of the pot to help keep the sap from bubbling over. Then he poured some sap into the pot, and as the sap boiled down, he added more.

Once it was done, they poured it into clean bottles. It was a lot of work for such a little bit of syrup, but they thought the effort was worth it, at least Kelly thought so.

Name ______________________ Date ________ Score ________

## Fluency MAZE Assessment

Kelly had been eagerly awaiting her favorite time of year. She checked the temperature every day **[mouth / until / socks]** at last, during the final week **[am / be / of]** March, the weather was warm enough. **[Key / The / Was]** family members put on warm clothes, **[gathered / possible / distract]** their supplies, and trekked into the **[woods / admit / later]**.

"Here's a tree that's big enough, Dad," Kelly **[author / inside / called].**

Everyone hurried over to join her. **[Help / They / Name]** checked the tree for old scars, **[ivy / for / and]** then Dad drilled three holes in **[the / ill / was]** bark and tapped in spouts. Kelly **[now / and / get]** her mom hung buckets on the **[affect / spouts / enough]** and covered them. Now all they **[had / you / job]** to do was wait for the **[reverse / awesome / buckets]** to fill with sap.

When the **[buckets / whistle / someday]** were full, they collected them and **[carried / involve / weather]** them back to the house. Dad **[ant / try / lit]** the fire in the outdoor fireplace. **[Know / They / Rely]** did not make syrup in the **[problem / kitchen / emotion]** because boiling sap made too much steam. **[My / He / Dad]** rubbed a little oil around the **[rim / and / yet]** of the pot to help keep **[can / win / the]** sap from bubbling over. Then he **[jumper / poured / public]** some sap into the pot, and **[he / as / up]** the sap boiled down, he added **[wish / play / more].**

Once it was done, they poured **[it / do / of]** into clean bottles. It was a **[cat / lot / but]** of work for such a little **[bit / all / end]** of syrup, but they thought **[top / hay / the]** effort was worth it, at least Kelly **[thought / struggle / fragile]** so.

Name ________________________ Date __________ Score __________

## Comprehension

**Read the following story. Then answer questions 1–10 relating to the story. You may look back at the story to find the answers.**

The kitchen smelled wonderful. Bill and his grandfather were making a huge pot of chili for the annual cook-off in the park. Bill watched as Pappy poured red pepper into his hand, looked at it, then added a bit more.

He poured each spice into his hand to judge how much to add. Today Bill had an idea. He asked Pappy to write down the recipe the next time he made chili. That way he could help, too.

A sad look crossed Pappy's face, and he shook his head. At first Bill thought Pappy did not want anyone to know his secret recipe, but that was not it. Pappy finally admitted he could not read or write. It had never occurred to Bill that Pappy could not read. "But you have the newspaper delivered," Bill protested, "and I've seen you reading it."

His grandfather reddened. "I only looked at the pictures. I could tell what most of the stories were from the television news. And you read me a lot of the others." When Bill asked his grandfather why he received the paper in the first place, Pappy gave a sheepish grin. "I couldn't have people thinking I was illiterate, now, could I?" He nudged Bill, "Pay attention to that chili, and don't let it burn!"



GO ON

## Comprehension (continued)

Bill scraped the bottom of the pot with the wooden spoon and went back to stirring the chili slowly. But his mind was bubbling with ideas. His grandfather had to work hard all his life to support his mother and younger brother and sister. But he was retired now, so he had plenty of time to learn.

"I never was very good at book learning," his grandfather said when Bill offered to teach him. "I don't think I'd be any good at reading."

"You won't know until you try," Bill said, repeating his grandfather's favorite saying.

"I guess it wouldn't hurt to try," Pappy said finally.

Bill pointed to the banner that stretched across the park entrance. But before he could tell his grandfather what each letter was, Pappy read the sign, "Timber City Annual Chili Cook-Off." Bill stared at him, and Pappy laughed. "I can't really read it. I just know what it says. When you were learning to read, you read it every year. I was so proud you could read all those words, I listened to every one."

Bill grinned. "If you remember everything I say that well, you'll be reading in no time."

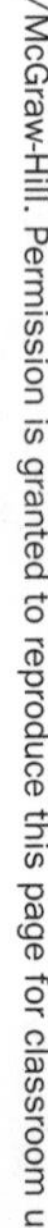


GO ON

## Comprehension (continued)

**1.** This story is mostly about

Ⓐ a boy discovering his grandfather's secret.

Ⓑ a grandfather teaching his grandson to cook.

Ⓒ a boy who wants to win a chili cook-off.

Ⓓ a grandfather who has a secret recipe.

**2.** Why did Pappy refuse to write down the recipe?

Ⓐ He could not remember the ingredients.

Ⓑ He would not share a family secret.

Ⓒ He did not know how to write.

Ⓓ He had trouble writing with his stiff hands.

**3.** Pappy had the newspaper delivered

Ⓐ so no one would know he could not read.

Ⓑ because he wanted to keep up with the world news.

Ⓒ to compare it to the stories on television.

Ⓓ because it gave Bill something to read.

**4.** What did Bill offer to do for Pappy?

Ⓐ take the chili to the park for him

Ⓑ teach Pappy how to read and write

Ⓒ help Pappy improve the chili recipe

Ⓓ stir the chili so it would not burn

**5.** How did Pappy first respond to Bill's offer?

Ⓐ He did not want to try new things.

Ⓑ He did not have enough time to do it.

Ⓒ He was not at all interested in learning.

Ⓓ He thought he would not be good at it.

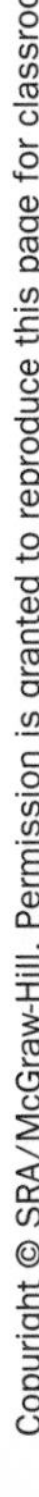


GO ON

## Comprehension (continued)

**6.** What did Bill ask Pappy to read?

Ⓐ a recipe from the chili cookbook

Ⓑ a story from that day's newspaper

Ⓒ a new book he had brought along

Ⓓ the sign for the Chili Cook-off

**7.** How did Pappy know what the words said?

Ⓐ Bill had read them to him before.

Ⓑ Pappy had seen them in another place.

Ⓒ Bill sounded out the words for Pappy.

Ⓓ Pappy sounded out each word.

**8.** From this story, you can tell that Bill

Ⓐ has never cooked chili before.

Ⓑ is very upset with his grandfather.

Ⓒ cares a lot about his grandfather.

Ⓓ will not win the Chili Cook-off.

**9.** Why do you think Pappy hid his secret from people?

Ⓐ It had just happened recently.

Ⓑ He was embarrassed about it.

Ⓒ He had always been very shy.

Ⓓ It was not important to him.

**10.** When Bill breathed the air in the kitchen, how might it have smelled?

Ⓐ very spicy

Ⓑ cool and lemony

Ⓒ sweet like candy

Ⓓ like spring flowers

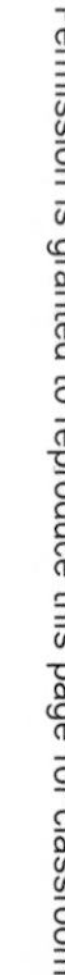


GO ON

## Comprehension

**Read the following selection. Then answer questions 1–10 relating to the selection. You may look back at the selection to find the answers.**

In England, huge rocks stand upright to form a large circle. It is called Stonehenge, and everyone wonders who built it and why. No one knows for sure, but it has been standing for thousands of years. Some parts may date from 8000 B.C. to 2000 B.C. The earliest parts were made of wood and earth. Later, large stones were added.

Inside the large circle of stones is a smaller one. The stones that make up these circles range from fourteen to twenty-four feet high. Some weigh almost twenty-five tons, while others weigh as much as fifty tons. The upright stones were cut so that other stones could be laid on top.

Many of the huge stones came from a quarry twenty-four miles away. Some stones, the bluestones, came from Wales. This is more than a hundred miles away. In 2001, some people tried to move stones the way people might have done it long ago. Using ropes and a wooden sled, they pulled a block of stone for miles. They even used special nets to make it easier, but it was still difficult to move. Then they loaded the stone onto a boat like those used in ancient times. This boat did not get far before it sank.



GO ON

## Comprehension (continued)

It is hard to imagine how all these stones could have been lifted and set in place. Some scientists think the stones may have been pushed there by glaciers. Others do not believe the stones would have come this far south. Even if the stones were nearby, lifting them was still a great feat. It must have taken millions of hours of work to complete it.

One man found a way to lift large stones upright without using modern machines. But the block he lifted was not as heavy as the ancient stones. To do it, people of long ago would need to know how to use levers and other tools. So how they built Stonehenge still remains a mystery.

Another mystery is why it was built. Some people think it was important for burying the dead. Many graves have been found in the area. Others think it predicted movements in the sun, moon, and stars. At sunrise and sunset long ago, the sun shone through the entrance. And on the longest day of the year, it would shine directly in the center. Although we may never know how or why it was made, Stonehenge is an interesting place to visit.



GO ON

## Comprehension (continued)

**1.** This selection is mostly about

Ⓐ why Stonehenge was built in ancient times.

Ⓑ who built Stonehenge and how they did it.

Ⓒ why Stonehenge still remains a mystery.

Ⓓ how all the huge stones got to Stonehenge.

**2.** When do scientists estimate that the earliest parts were built?

Ⓐ 8000 B.C. to 2000 B.C.

Ⓑ 30,000 B.C. to 20,000 B.C.

Ⓒ 1000 A.D. to 1500 A.D.

Ⓓ 200 B.C. to 800 A.D.

**3.** How did the earlier parts differ from the later parts?

Ⓐ First stones were put in a circle, then mounds were added.

Ⓑ First the stones were put up, then wood was added.

Ⓒ First people lived there, then they buried people there.

Ⓓ First it was wood and earth, then the stones were added.

**4.** Where did the bluestones come from?

Ⓐ from the nearby mountains and lakes

Ⓑ from a hundred miles away in Wales

Ⓒ from glaciers shaping them long ago

Ⓓ from a quarry twenty-four miles away

**5.** When huge stones were put on a model of an ancient boat in 2001,

Ⓐ the boat floated low in the water.

Ⓑ the stones arrived a few at a time.

Ⓒ the boat sank after it was loaded.

Ⓓ the stones could not fit on deck.

## Comprehension (continued)

**6.** To build Stonehenge, people did NOT need to know

Ⓐ where to find all the large stones.

Ⓑ how to transport such heavy stones.

Ⓒ how to lift such heavy loads.

Ⓓ how to lay bricks to build houses.

**7.** The reason some people believe Stonehenge was a burial ground is that

Ⓐ the stones have dates on them.

Ⓑ bodies are buried in the area.

Ⓒ they found many burial tools.

Ⓓ old records show it was.

**8.** What do some people believe Stonehenge was used for?

Ⓐ predicting movements of bodies in space

Ⓑ as a quarry for digging up huge stones

Ⓒ a port for transporting goods by boat

Ⓓ an ancient village of homes and stores

**9.** From this selection, you can tell that the builders of Stonehenge

Ⓐ used very primitive building methods.

Ⓑ did not make it very well, as it is now in ruins.

Ⓒ did something that was very difficult.

Ⓓ knew very little about how to work with stone.

**10.** A good title for this selection is

Ⓐ "Ancient Machines."

Ⓑ "Rock Climbing."

Ⓒ "The Mysteries of Stonehenge."

Ⓓ "A Visit to England."

## Vocabulary

**Read each item. Fill in the bubble for the answer you think is correct.**

**1.** Disagree means

Ⓐ move over.

Ⓑ line up.

Ⓒ respect.

Ⓓ differ.

**2.** Produce is the base word in overproduction. Overproduction means

Ⓐ full of pain.

Ⓑ more than needed.

Ⓒ without money.

Ⓓ almost finished.

**3.** A telescope helps you

Ⓐ see things that are far away.

Ⓑ hear things that are said softly.

Ⓒ speak to people across the world.

Ⓓ write letters and notes.

**4.** What word means about the same as filthy?

Ⓐ happy

Ⓑ spotless

Ⓒ dirty

Ⓓ tired

**5.** What word means about the same as handy?

Ⓐ hopeless

Ⓑ clumsy

Ⓒ busy

Ⓓ useful

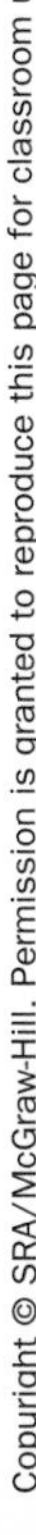


GO ON

## Vocabulary (continued)

**6.** What word means the opposite of bitter?

Ⓐ earlier
Ⓑ salty
Ⓒ happy
Ⓓ harsh

**7.** Which word BEST completes both sentences?

**The school ___ met yesterday.**

**Please hand me the ___ I just cut.**

Ⓐ group
Ⓑ board
Ⓒ log
Ⓓ committee

**8.** Which word BEST completes both sentences?

**The runner began to ___.**

**That ___ is still a little low.**

Ⓐ sweat
Ⓑ car
Ⓒ tire
Ⓓ turn

**9.** The ice storm made the trip home perilous. Perilous means

Ⓐ blinding.
Ⓑ dangerous.
Ⓒ long.
Ⓓ slippery.

**10.** Since his directions were vague, we got lost. Vague means

Ⓐ spoken.
Ⓑ good.
Ⓒ long.
Ⓓ unclear.

STOP

## Grammar, Usage, and Mechanics

**Read each question. Fill in the bubble beside the answer in each group that is correct. If none of the answers is correct, choose the last answer, "none of the above."**

**1.** Which sentence is written correctly?

Ⓐ My Mother and I visited the statue of liberty and ellis island, New York.

Ⓑ My mother and I visited the Statue of liberty and Ellis island, New York.

Ⓒ My mother and I visited the statue of liberty and Ellis Island, New York.

Ⓓ none of the above

**2.** Which sentence is written incorrectly?

Ⓐ Mom put these on her shopping list apples, grapes, cheese, and milk.

Ⓑ We have to play these teams twice: the Tigers, the Lions, and the Bears.

Ⓒ I ate a big lunch; Charles hardly ate at all.

Ⓓ none of the above

**3.** Which sentence is written correctly?

Ⓐ Please do not eat none cookies before dinner.

Ⓑ Please do not eat any cookies before dinner.

Ⓒ Please do not eat no cookies before dinner.

Ⓓ none of the above

**4.** Which sentence is written correctly?

Ⓐ The guide said, "to enter, please use the other door.

Ⓑ The guide said, "To enter", "please use the other door."

Ⓒ The guide said, "To enter, please use the other door."

Ⓓ none of the above

**5.** Which sentence is written incorrectly?

Ⓐ This computer is larger than that one.

Ⓑ This computer is the most expensive one.

Ⓒ This computer is most expensive than that one.

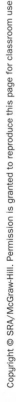

Ⓓ none of the above

GO ON

## Grammar, Usage, and Mechanics (continued)

**6.** Which sentence is written correctly?

Ⓐ In ancient China, only emperors were allowed to wear yellow.

Ⓑ Only emperors in ancient China was allowed to wear yellow.

Ⓒ In ancient China, only emperors was allowed to wear yellow.

Ⓓ none of the above

**7.** Which sentence is written correctly?

Ⓐ You can help yourself to them salad and bread.

Ⓑ You can help yourself to their salad and bread.

Ⓒ You can help you to they salad and bread.

Ⓓ none of the above

**8.** Which sentence is written correctly?

Ⓐ Josh will handle the film, and Jim carried the camera.

Ⓑ Josh handled the film, and Jim carries the camera.

Ⓒ Josh will handle the film, and Jim will carry the camera.

Ⓓ none of the above

**9.** Which sentence is written correctly?

Ⓐ Five people with their bags beside them.

Ⓑ The train to Paris and also to London.

Ⓒ The people's large suitcases and many other packages.

Ⓓ none of the above

**10.** What type of sentence is this?

**Penny has played soccer for many years, and we think she should be captain.**

Ⓐ Simple

Ⓑ Compound

Ⓒ Complex

Ⓓ Not a sentence

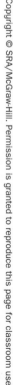

STOP

## Spelling

**Read each group of words. Only one of the words is spelled correctly. Fill in the bubble under the word that is spelled correctly.**

| | | | | |
|---|---|---|---|---|
| **1.** | activities | aktivities | asctiveties | activiteis |
| | Ⓐ | Ⓑ | Ⓒ | Ⓓ |
| **2.** | eccsuse | ecuse | excuse | axcuse |
| | Ⓐ | Ⓑ | Ⓒ | Ⓓ |
| **3.** | campayn | campaign | cempaign | campain |
| | Ⓐ | Ⓑ | Ⓒ | Ⓓ |
| **4.** | ativate | activat | actavate | activate |
| | Ⓐ | Ⓑ | Ⓒ | Ⓓ |
| **5.** | plainly | playnley | planly | palinly |
| | Ⓐ | Ⓑ | Ⓒ | Ⓓ |



GO ON

## Spelling (continued)

**In each sentence, look for the underlined word that is spelled incorrectly. Focus on just the underlined word. Fill in the bubble next to the sentence with the misspelled word. If all the underlined words are spelled correctly, choose "correct as is."**

6. Ⓐ The fabric for the curtain is sheer.
   Ⓑ Instructions are attached to the new television.
   Ⓒ Waiting for Trey delayed us.
   Ⓓ correct as is

7. Ⓐ José gave a groan when they scored.
   Ⓑ Dyan let me borrow her new sweatter.
   Ⓒ The baseball flew through the window pane.
   Ⓓ correct as is

8. Ⓐ The gravel road was bumpy.
   Ⓑ Our class wants to publish a newsletter.
   Ⓒ A pencil and notebook are esential for taking notes.
   Ⓓ correct as is

9. Ⓐ Pete drew cars and monsters on his paper.
   Ⓑ Susan mowed the grass for the neighbors.
   Ⓒ Smelling flowers makes Brian sneaze.
   Ⓓ correct as is

10. Ⓐ Tomato juice helps with a skunk's oder.
    Ⓑ Hiking this trail can be difficult.
    Ⓒ Dad saw if the locks were secure.
    Ⓓ correct as is

**This is the end of the group-administered section of the Benchmark Assessment.**

**Name** ______________________ **Date** __________ **Score** __________

# Oral Fluency Assessment

Things kept disappearing. Mary thought there must be 1–8
a thief in the neighborhood. First it was Aunt Becky's pie 9–19
left on the porch ledge to cool. The pan had been licked 20–31
clean and then dropped on the porch. Next, it was a basket 32–43
of apples. The thief was in a hurry because pieces of apple 44–55
were still on the ground. Mary followed the trail to the grass 56–67
and studied the ground like she'd seen detectives do on 68–77
television, but found no more evidence. The thief must have 78–87
gone through the grass toward the barnyard or pasture. She 88–97
searched the dusty ground for footprints, but only found 98–106
chicken tracks and goat hoof prints, and those were 107–115
always there. 116–117

There had to be a way to find out who was stealing 118–129
things. The only thing the two crimes had in common was 130–140
that they were related to food, so Mary decided to trap the 141–152
thief with food. 153–155

Early the next morning, Mary put some fruit on a plate 156–166
and set it on the ledge, then crouched down inside to wait. 167–178
Suddenly, the plate crashed to the porch. Mary rushed to the 179–189
window in time to see one of the goats trotting off the porch. 190–202
She had solved the mystery, and all that was left was to 203–214
convince Aunt Becky to stop putting food on the windowsill. 215–224

**READING RATE AND ACCURACY**

Total Words Read: ____

Number of Errors: ____

Number of Correct Words
Read Per Minute (WPM): ____

Accuracy Rate: ____

(Number of Correct Words Read per Minute ÷ Total Words Read)

**READING FLUENCY**

| | Low | Average | High |
|---|---|---|---|
| Decoding Ability | ○ | ○ | ○ |
| Pace | ○ | ○ | ○ |
| Syntax | ○ | ○ | ○ |
| Self-correction | ○ | ○ | ○ |
| Intonation | ○ | ○ | ○ |

## Oral Fluency Assessment

Things kept disappearing. Mary thought there must be a thief in the neighborhood. First it was Aunt Becky's pie left on the porch ledge to cool. The pan had been licked clean and then dropped on the porch. Next, it was a basket of apples. The thief was in a hurry because pieces of apple were still on the ground. Mary followed the trail to the grass and studied the ground like she'd seen detectives do on television, but found no more evidence. The thief must have gone through the grass toward the barnyard or pasture. She searched the dusty ground for footprints, but only found chicken tracks and goat hoof prints, and those were always there.

There had to be a way to find out who was stealing things. The only thing the two crimes had in common was that they were related to food, so Mary decided to trap the thief with food.

Early the next morning, Mary put some fruit on a plate and set it on the ledge, then crouched down inside to wait. Suddenly, the plate crashed to the porch. Mary rushed to the window in time to see one of the goats trotting off the porch. She had solved the mystery, and all that was left was to convince Aunt Becky to stop putting food on the windowsill.

Name ______________________ Date ________ Score ________

## Fluency MAZE Assessment

Things kept disappearing. Mary thought there must be a **[purse / thief / add]** in the neighborhood. First it was Aunt Becky's pie **[left / feel / rush]** on the porch ledge to cool. **[The / Gap / Use]** pan had been licked clean and **[stay / hand / then]** dropped on the porch. Next, it **[lie / was / rub]** a basket of apples. The thief **[was / toy / ram]** in a hurry because pieces of **[ready / meant / apple ]** were still on the ground. Mary **[diplomat / followed / presence]** the trail to the grass and **[incline / perfect / studied]** the ground like she'd seen detectives **[at / do / me]** on television, but found no more **[backfire / evidence / decision]**. The thief must have gone through **[the / fur / pal]** grass toward the barnyard or pasture. **[Fun / Lip / She]** searched the dusty ground for footprints, **[its / but / zoo]** only found chicken tracks and goat **[hoof / knew / lean]** prints, and those were always there.

**[There / Ready / Chest]** had to be a way to **[last / wild / find]** out who was stealing things. The **[only / rely / were]** thing the two crimes had in **[common / nation / across]** was that they were related to food, so Mary **[experts / balance / decided]** to trap the thief with food.

**[Guess / Blame / Early]** the next morning, Mary put some **[truck / fruit / blame]** on a plate and set it on **[the / than / because]** ledge, then crouched down inside **[to / up / we]** wait. Suddenly, the plate crashed to **[bay / one / the]** porch. Mary rushed to the window **[as / in / by]** time to see one of the **[meant / about / goats]** trotting off the porch. She had **[solved / couple / choice]** the mystery, and all that was **[miss / rush / left]** was to convince Aunt Becky to **[till / stop / adds]** putting food on the windowsill.

Name ______________________________ Date __________ Score __________

## Comprehension

**Read the following story. Then answer questions 1–10 relating to the story. You may look back at the story to find the answers.**

Semir was glad to get an invitation to Jenna's party. He had only been in America a little over a year. But he was making friends. The week before the party, he and his friend Erik went shopping together to buy something for Jenna. With Erik's help, Semir picked out a gift and a card.

Semir walked to the party alone because Erik had gone to his brother's basketball game. Erik's dad would drop him off later. Semir knew the present should be a surprise. Erik had explained that to him, so he left it in the store bag. That way Jenna would not see it.

When Jenna opened the door and showed him where to put the present, Semir's smile faded. All the other presents were in fancy boxes with shiny ribbons on them. Why had Erik not told him that?

Semir stood in the doorway of the next room, watching. Everyone seemed to be in small groups. There was food on a table, but he was not sure if he should help himself or wait until someone invited him to eat. He looked around, but Jenna was greeting people at the door.



GO ON

## Comprehension (continued)

Erik arrived just before Jenna opened her gifts. She opened Semir's bag first and made a remark about the original wrapping paper. People started to laugh, but Erik cut in.

"Hey, the gift's the important thing, right? You only throw away the paper anyway."

Jenna nodded and reached in the bag. She looked puzzled as she pulled out the unsigned card, then its blank envelope.

"That is so you can recycle it," Erik told her. He leaned toward Semir. "Sorry, I should have told you that."

Jenna thanked Semir for the gift. As she opened the other gifts, Semir realized that everyone had signed the cards and put them inside the envelopes.

As they walked out the door, Semir told Erik how embarrassed he was, but Erik told him not to worry about it. "It is not easy to learn all these new things," Erik said. "You'll catch on. It just takes time."

Jenna overheard them and ran out beside them. "Semir, that was a wonderful gift. We sometimes don't think about the customs we take for granted. I'm going to make sure that all of us help you understand things better. I'll walk part of the way home with you two so we can just talk."

## Comprehension (continued)

**1.** This story is mostly about

Ⓐ a boy trying to learn new customs.

Ⓑ how to wrap a birthday gift properly.

Ⓒ why people are sometimes impatient.

Ⓓ a boy who learns a new language.

**2.** Erik and Semir go shopping for

Ⓐ basketball uniforms.

Ⓑ wrapping paper.

Ⓒ Jenna's present.

Ⓓ a birthday cake.

**3.** Why did Erik not go to the party with Semir?

Ⓐ He went there early to help Jenna decorate.

Ⓑ His parents did not allow him to go to parties.

Ⓒ He was going there with his other friends.

Ⓓ He went to his brother's basketball game first.

**4.** How did Semir wrap the gift to surprise Jenna?

Ⓐ He used fancy paper and bows.

Ⓑ He left it in the store bag.

Ⓒ He decorated a special box.

Ⓓ He got a birthday gift bag.

**5.** Why was Jenna surprised by Semir's card?

Ⓐ He had picked one that made her laugh.

Ⓑ It was written in another language.

Ⓒ His card was bigger than all the others.

Ⓓ It was not signed or in its envelope.

## Comprehension (continued)

6. Erik tried to make Semir feel better in all these ways EXCEPT
   - Ⓐ he told everyone the card could be recycled.
   - Ⓑ he apologized for not explaining about cards.
   - Ⓒ he invited him to play basketball with him.
   - Ⓓ he said wrapping paper was only thrown away.

7. From this story, you can tell that Erik
   - Ⓐ was a kind and caring person.
   - Ⓑ preferred basketball to parties.
   - Ⓒ did not know Jenna very well.
   - Ⓓ did not have many friends.

8. At the end, Jenna realized that it was
   - Ⓐ time for everyone to leave.
   - Ⓑ hard to make friends.
   - Ⓒ fun to get so many gifts.
   - Ⓓ difficult to learn new customs.

9. How did Semir feel when Jenna opened her other gifts and cards?
   - Ⓐ jealous that Jenna got them
   - Ⓑ embarrassed about his mistake
   - Ⓒ happy that she got nice gifts
   - Ⓓ curious to see what she got

10. What will Semir, Jenna, and Erik probably talk about during the walk home?
    - Ⓐ basketball
    - Ⓑ school subjects
    - Ⓒ other customs
    - Ⓓ Jenna's gifts

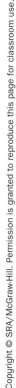

## Comprehension

**Read the following selection. Then answer questions 1–10 relating to the selection. You may look back at the selection to find the answers.**

At one time, it was not easy for women to be inventors. For centuries, men took credit for things their wives or daughters thought up. Still, women came up with many new ideas. A few even patented them. A patent is a legal document that shows who thought of an invention.

Getting a patent is not easy. First you must have an idea that is a new one. The idea has to work and be useful. Next you must prove that you are the first person to think of this idea. A dated journal can help prove when and how you worked out and tested your idea. You also have to show that the idea works. It is best to have a small model of it, too.

These steps take time. They can also be costly. The steps kept many women from getting patents over the years. Finding the time and money to patent their ideas was hard. Most women had no way to do real research. They could not know if someone else had already made their ideas.

Also, few women had money of their own. Anything they owned belonged to their husbands. So it was rare for a woman to be able to get a patent for something she had done. It was not until 1809 that the first woman got a patent.



GO ON

## Comprehension (continued)

By 1840, only twenty women had patents. Most of these were for things you would find in the house. These things improved clothing, cooking tools, or stoves. Several of these patents updated the iron, sewing thread, and the weaving process. These ideas were all things women could test in their homes.

Few women spent time thinking up ideas to make machines work better. Women were not supposed to know much about machinery or how it worked. And if they did, most of them did not admit it. This did not stop Sarah Mather. She came up with an unusual idea for her time. She had an idea for a submarine telescope and lamp.

Little is known about her life. There is no sure way to know how she knew about telescopes. It is very surprising that she could design one. It was to be used beneath the water to check the depth of the ocean. Still, she did come up with the idea. She even went to the trouble to patent it in 1845. It makes you wonder how many other great finds women could have made if they had been able to patent their ideas over the years.



GO ON

## Comprehension (continued)

**1.** This selection is mostly about

Ⓐ the many different engines women invented.

Ⓑ the difficulties women had getting patents.

Ⓒ how to do the research needed for a patent.

Ⓓ why few women had money of their own.

**2.** What happened to many women's inventions long ago?

Ⓐ Their patents were never recorded.

Ⓑ Most of them did not work well.

Ⓒ Women never invented anything.

Ⓓ Men often took credit for them.

**3.** Which of these is NOT needed for a patent?

Ⓐ proof that you are the first to think of the idea

Ⓑ drawings to show how the invention works

Ⓒ proof that the idea works and will be useful

Ⓓ a bill showing how much it will cost to make

**4.** Why did most women invent household items?

Ⓐ They were not allowed to do other things.

Ⓑ Most women worked in the home.

Ⓒ Men never invented anything for the home.

Ⓓ There was no need for other types of inventions.

**5.** Attitudes toward women affected how many patents they got by

Ⓐ making them feel it was unacceptable to invent things.

Ⓑ encouraging them to learn about engines and science.

Ⓒ teaching them to take credit for the things they made.

Ⓓ giving them many opportunities to try new things.

## Comprehension (continued)

6. Women did not get patents for all these reasons EXCEPT

   Ⓐ it was too expensive.

   Ⓑ only men could get patents.

   Ⓒ they mainly stayed home.

   Ⓓ they could not do research.

7. What did Sarah Mather design?

   Ⓐ a submarine telescope and lamp

   Ⓑ a machine to wash dishes

   Ⓒ a steering device for a boat

   Ⓓ a sonar detector for the ocean

8. From this selection, you can tell that women who got patents

   Ⓐ did not do anything with their patents.

   Ⓑ had a hard time selling their inventions.

   Ⓒ could not have a home and family, too.

   Ⓓ had to overcome many obstacles.

9. Women were likely to get patents for all these things EXCEPT

   Ⓐ better clothing and stoves.

   Ⓑ new sewing thread and irons.

   Ⓒ a new weaving process.

   Ⓓ car and truck engines.

10. Sarah Mather's invention was unique because

    Ⓐ women could only design things for their houses.

    Ⓑ no one knows much about her or her life.

    Ⓒ most women then did not know about machines.

    Ⓓ she had no opportunity to research patents.

## Vocabulary

**Read each item. Fill in the bubble for the answer you think is correct.**

**1.** Descendant means

Ⓐ a group that protects old buildings.

Ⓑ a scientist who studies the deep ocean.

Ⓒ a person related to a person in the past.

Ⓓ a meeting that took place long ago.

**2.** Obey is the base word in disobey. Disobey means

Ⓐ leave a place.

Ⓑ not follow a rule.

Ⓒ meet with.

Ⓓ do something twice.

**3.** A biography is

Ⓐ a life story.

Ⓑ the science of life.

Ⓒ a math formula.

Ⓓ a machine.

**4.** What word means about the same as condensed?

Ⓐ extended

Ⓑ perplexed

Ⓒ attached

Ⓓ shortened

**5.** What word means about the same as slack?

Ⓐ shiny

Ⓑ complete

Ⓒ loose

Ⓓ tight

## Vocabulary (continued)

**6.** What word means the opposite of definitely?

Ⓐ possibly
Ⓑ surely
Ⓒ thoroughly
Ⓓ lately

**7.** Which word BEST completes both sentences?

**I can finish it in a ___.**

**The lightning ___ frightened us.**

Ⓐ hurry
Ⓑ bolt
Ⓒ flash
Ⓓ rod

**8.** Which word BEST completes both sentences?

**Allen ___ a hole into the wood.**

**We were ___ waiting for the train.**

Ⓐ drilled
Ⓑ cold
Ⓒ bored
Ⓓ busy

**9.** The modest girl did not want to accept the award. Modest means

Ⓐ shy.
Ⓑ little.
Ⓒ sleepy.
Ⓓ pretty.

**10.** Many children are transported to school by a bus. Transported means

Ⓐ carried.
Ⓑ accepted.
Ⓒ attached.
Ⓓ helped.

STOP

## Grammar, Usage, and Mechanics

**Read each question. Fill in the bubble beside the answer in each group that is correct. If none of the answers is correct, choose the last answer, "none of the above."**

**1.** Which sentence is written correctly?

Ⓐ Mexico's Independence Day is September 15.

Ⓑ Mexico's Independence day is September 15.

Ⓒ Mexico's independence day is September 15.

Ⓓ none of the above

**2.** Which sentence is written correctly?

Ⓐ We lost however, Coach still took us for pizza.

Ⓑ We lost; however, Coach still took us for pizza.

Ⓒ We lost: however, Coach still took us for pizza.

Ⓓ none of the above

**3.** Which sentence is written <u>incorrectly</u>?

Ⓐ I cannot find any books on car racing.

Ⓑ I have not read one for a long time.

Ⓒ This library does not have none of those books.

Ⓓ none of the above

**4.** Which sentence is written <u>incorrectly</u>?

Ⓐ Mother said, "You have a piano lesson."

Ⓑ Mona asked, "what day is my piano lesson?"

Ⓒ "Your lessons are on Tuesday," Mother replied.

Ⓓ none of the above

**5.** Which sentence is written correctly?

Ⓐ Everyone listened more carefully to George.

Ⓑ Everyone listened more careful to George.

Ⓒ Everyone listened most carefuller to George.

Ⓓ none of the above

GO ON

## Grammar, Usage, and Mechanics (continued)

**6.** Which sentence is written correctly?

Ⓐ Herb were blowing a whistle to call everyone together.

Ⓑ Herb, to call everyone together, were blowing a whistle.

Ⓒ To call everyone together, Herb was blowing a whistle.

Ⓓ none of the above

**7.** Which sentence is written correctly?

Ⓐ I and Devon went shopping at the mall.

Ⓑ Devon and me went shopping at the mall.

Ⓒ Me and Devon went shopping at the mall.

Ⓓ none of the above

**8.** Which sentence is written correctly?

Ⓐ Mom uses the machine outside when the lines were too long in the bank.

Ⓑ Lines inside the bank will be too long, so Mom used the machine outside.

Ⓒ Lines inside the bank were too long, so Mom used the machine outside.

Ⓓ none of the above

**9.** Which sentence is written correctly?

Ⓐ Too much water in the air and warm weather in summer.

Ⓑ Before the storm began, black clouds formed overhead.

Ⓒ Huge black clouds heavy with plenty of raindrops.

Ⓓ none of the above

**10.** What type of sentence is this?

**That glass and this pitcher need to be washed and dried.**

Ⓐ Simple

Ⓑ Compound

Ⓒ Complex

Ⓓ Not a sentence

## Spelling

**Read each group of words. Only one of the words is spelled correctly. Fill in the bubble under the word that is spelled correctly.**

| | | | | |
|---|---|---|---|---|
| **1.** | socs | socks | sokcs | soks |
| | Ⓐ | Ⓑ | Ⓒ | Ⓓ |
| **2.** | curtian | cutrain | curtain | crutain |
| | Ⓐ | Ⓑ | Ⓒ | Ⓓ |
| **3.** | drizel | drizzel | drizzul | drizzle |
| | Ⓐ | Ⓑ | Ⓒ | Ⓓ |
| **4.** | bowndry | boundary | boondary | boyndary |
| | Ⓐ | Ⓑ | Ⓒ | Ⓓ |
| **5.** | spacecraft | spacecarft | spacecraf | spasecraft |
| | Ⓐ | Ⓑ | Ⓒ | Ⓓ |



GO ON

## Spelling (continued)

**In each sentence, look for the underlined word that is spelled incorrectly. Focus on just the underlined word. Fill in the bubble next to the sentence with the misspelled word. If all the underlined words are spelled correctly, choose "correct as is."**

**6.** Ⓐ It took fifteen gallons of gasoline to fill the tank.
Ⓑ The distance to town is about ten miles.
Ⓒ Some medicines may cause diziness.
Ⓓ correct as is

**7.** Ⓐ Paul is accustomed to waiting for Drew.
Ⓑ Do you like this pattern for the chair covers?
Ⓒ Vera claims she should go first.
Ⓓ correct as is

**8.** Ⓐ Deb bought material for a new dress.
Ⓑ Would you like to go for a sliegh ride?
Ⓒ Mia debates on our school team.
Ⓓ correct as is

**9.** Ⓐ The new worker had prior experience.
Ⓑ The park is public property.
Ⓒ Did you relize it is time to go?
Ⓓ correct as is

**10.** Ⓐ Can I depend on you to finish the job?
Ⓑ Latoya picked out the perfume.
Ⓒ The beating of the heart is automatic.
Ⓓ correct as is

**This is the end of the group-administered section of the Benchmark Assessment.**

**Name** ________________ **Date** ________ **Score** ________

# Oral Fluency Assessment

It is a dark night in Scotland. The water of Loch Ness is 1–13
calm and black. Suddenly, a strange rippling appears on the 14–23
water. A huge figure rises out of the water. It is the Loch Ness 24–37
monster! Or is it? 38–41

The mystery of what may live in the Scottish lake Loch 42–52
Ness has held the imagination of the world for a long time. 53–64
Local parents told their children that the monster would get 65–74
them if they played too close to the shores of the lake. But the 75–88
recent Nessie mania started in 1933. It was then that a couple 89–100
traveling along a road near the shore decided to take a photo. 101–112
This photo is thought of as the first look at the monster. 113–124

Since then many others have claimed to have seen the 125–134
beast. People have captured strange images in pictures 135–142
and on video. Some have recorded odd sounds they say 143–152
were made by Nessie. In recent years, explorers have used 153–162
submarines and radar equipment to find the elusive monster. 163–171
So far, though, no one has been able to prove that a huge 172–184
beast lives in the lake. Every once in a while someone will 185–196
take a picture or shoot a film that seems to confirm Nessie's 197–208
existence. Maybe the monster really exists. Maybe it does not. 209–218
One day we may know for sure. 219–225

**READING RATE AND ACCURACY**

Total Words Read: ____

Number of Errors: ____

Number of Correct Words Read Per Minute (WPM): ____

Accuracy Rate: ____

(Number of Correct Words Read per Minute ÷ Total Words Read)

**READING FLUENCY**

| | Low | Average | High |
|---|---|---|---|
| Decoding Ability | ○ | ○ | ○ |
| Pace | ○ | ○ | ○ |
| Syntax | ○ | ○ | ○ |
| Self-correction | ○ | ○ | ○ |
| Intonation | ○ | ○ | ○ |

## Oral Fluency Assessment

It is a dark night in Scotland. The water of Loch Ness is calm and black. Suddenly, a strange rippling appears on the water. A huge figure rises out of the water. It is the Loch Ness monster! Or is it?

The mystery of what may live in the Scottish lake Loch Ness has held the imagination of the world for a long time. Local parents told their children that the monster would get them if they played too close to the shores of the lake. But the recent Nessie mania started in 1933. It was then that a couple traveling along a road near the shore decided to take a photo. This photo is thought of as the first look at the monster.

Since then many others have claimed to have seen the beast. People have captured strange images in pictures and on video. Some have recorded odd sounds they say were made by Nessie. In recent years, explorers have used submarines and radar equipment to find the elusive monster. So far, though, no one has been able to prove that a huge beast lives in the lake. Every once in a while someone will take a picture or shoot a film that seems to confirm Nessie's existence. Maybe the monster really exists. Maybe it does not. One day we may know for sure.

**Name** ______________________ **Date** __________ **Score** __________

## Fluency MAZE Assessment

It is a dark night in Scotland. The water of Loch Ness is calm and **[black / year / when]**. Suddenly, a strange rippling appears on **[the / sop / fit]** water. A huge figure rises out **[it / of / be]** the water. It is the Loch Ness **[monster / broader / passing]**! Or is it?

The mystery of **[mind / cast / what]** may live in the Scottish lake Loch Ness **[joy / tax / has]** held the imagination of the world **[six / for / hay]** a long time. Local parents told **[smile / their / toast]** children that the monster would get **[them / wild / lean]** if they played too close **[me / to / am]** the shores of the lake. But **[gum / fox / the]** recent Nessie mania started in 1933. It **[was / to / am]** then that a couple traveling along a **[road / plane / jump]** near the shore decided to take a **[lake / shoe / photo]**. This photo is thought of as the **[first / must / beast]** look at the monster.

Since then many **[winter / others / memory]** have claimed to have seen the **[beast / tried / threw]**. People have captured strange images in **[decision / reviewed / pictures]** and on video. Some have recorded **[odd / too / pun]** sounds they say were made by Nessie. **[Am / In / Or]** recent years, explorers have used submarines **[and / key / had]** radar equipment to find the elusive **[dreamed / monster / explain]**. So far, though, no one has **[last / goes / been]** able to prove that a huge **[beast / because / thought]** lives in the lake. Every once **[go / as / in]** a while someone will take a **[perfect / picture / conclude]** or shoot a film that seems **[to / me / us]** confirm Nessie's existence. Maybe the monster **[silent / really / better]** exists. Maybe it does not. One day **[so / up / we]** may know for sure.

# Expository Writing Prompt

## Writing Situation

Think about a house you would like to have when you grow up. Tell about the different parts of the house, such as the kitchen and the living room. Describe where the house would be built and what the outside would look like. Explain why this house would be your dream house.

## Checklist

You will earn the best score if you

- think about the house fully and plan your writing before you begin.
- make sure your ideas flow in a way that makes sense to your audience.
- provide details so the reader can understand what the house and its surroundings look like.
- use sensory words and descriptive language to describe the house.
- clearly explain why this is your dream house.
- connect the sections of your writing so that nothing seems out of place.
- use correct capital letters, punctuation, and spelling.
- use subjects, verbs, and modifiers correctly.
- write complete sentences and avoid fragments or run-ons.
- read your writing after you finish and check for mistakes.

# Benchmark 1 Answer Sheets



**Comprehension (continued)**

1. This story is mostly about
   - ● a girl who was afraid to do announcements.
   - Ⓑ a boy who missed school because he was sick.
   - Ⓒ a teacher who made students read the announcements.
   - Ⓓ a boy who had a sore throat and could not talk.
2. Why does Jamie get to school at the last minute?
   - Ⓐ She does not want to meet Art in the hall.
   - ● She does not want to do the announcements.
   - Ⓒ She forgot her homework and has to get it.
   - Ⓓ She misses the bus and has to walk to school.
3. Why does Jamie not want to do the announcements?
   - Ⓐ She does not think it is her turn yet.
   - Ⓑ She does not read very well.
   - ● She is nervous about it.
   - Ⓓ She will miss her favorite class.
4. Why is Jamie glad to see Art at school?
   - ● She thinks he will do announcements.
   - Ⓑ She has been worried about Art's health.
   - Ⓒ She and Art have plans after school that day.
   - Ⓓ She wants someone to sit with at lunch.
5. Why does Mr. Martin tell Jamie to go to the office?
   - Ⓐ She is late for school that morning.
   - Ⓑ He wants her to take a note to the principal.
   - ● She needs to take Art's place.
   - Ⓓ There is a phone call for her in the office.

**Benchmark 1**



**Comprehension (continued)**

6. What advice does the school secretary give Jamie?
   - Ⓐ Pretend you are in your bedroom.
   - Ⓑ Do not look at the pages when you read.
   - ● Pretend no one else is listening.
   - Ⓓ Speak loudly and clearly.
7. What does Jamie do before she starts to read?
   - Ⓐ She looks over the paper.
   - ● She clears her throat.
   - Ⓒ She reads aloud to herself.
   - Ⓓ She turns on the mike.
8. From this story, you can tell that Mr. Martin
   - Ⓐ is very strict with his students.
   - Ⓑ worries that his students might fail.
   - Ⓒ wants his students to pay attention.
   - ● tries to encourage his students.
9. What happens to Jamie after she starts reading?
   - Ⓐ Her voice gets high and squeaky.
   - ● Her nervousness passes.
   - Ⓒ Her hands shake badly.
   - Ⓓ Her eyesight is blurry.
10. How might Jamie have felt once the announcements were over?
    - ● relieved, but proud
    - Ⓑ sad and frightened
    - Ⓒ glad, but worried
    - Ⓓ uncertain and nervous

**Benchmark 1**



**Comprehension (continued)**

1. This story is mostly about
   - Ⓐ the dams in creeks near sand dunes.
   - Ⓑ the wildlife that live on sand dunes.
   - Ⓒ the waterfalls near some sand dunes.
   - ● the development of big sand dunes.
2. What is most unusual about the Great Sand Dunes?
   - Ⓐ They have many kinds of wildlife on them.
   - ● They are not anywhere near the ocean.
   - Ⓒ It took a long time for them to be formed.
   - Ⓓ Their shapes are still changing every day.
3. Which of these helped form the Great Sand Dunes initially?
   - Ⓐ mountains that eroded over a long time
   - Ⓑ rivers that carried sand away from beaches
   - Ⓒ water that evaporated and formed sand
   - ● rock under ash from volcanoes that erupted.
4. Which of these does NOT help barchan dunes form?
   - Ⓐ The wind's path is not blocked by anything.
   - Ⓑ The wind must blow straight ahead.
   - Ⓒ The wind scoops out the center of the sand.
   - ● The wind blows sand over creeks.
5. Parabolic dunes are formed by wind blowing
   - Ⓐ in a straight line.
   - Ⓑ in two directions.
   - ● around the plants.
   - Ⓓ up instead of down.

**Benchmark 1**



**Comprehension (continued)**

6. What causes surges in the creek?
   - Ⓐ lightning hitting the water
   - ● water knocking over sand dams
   - Ⓒ heavy rains that overfill the creek
   - Ⓓ waterfalls flooding the creek
7. How were the dunes shaped and changed?
   - Ⓐ by the movement of earthquakes
   - Ⓑ by ancient people digging there
   - Ⓒ by waterfalls dripping on the sand
   - ● by the movement of the wind
8. From this selection, you can tell that the dunes
   - ● are still being shaped by the winds.
   - Ⓑ are slowly eroding and getting flat.
   - Ⓒ are not a good place for plants to grow.
   - Ⓓ are not a very safe place to visit.
9. Why are some rare forms of wildlife found in the dunes?
   - ● It is an unusual habitat, so animals adapted to it.
   - Ⓑ They have been brought here by the wind.
   - Ⓒ Scientists introduced them here as an experiment.
   - Ⓓ Zoos have bred new wildlife in this area.
10. Why do hikers follow the dune's ridgelines?
    - Ⓐ They do not want to fall.
    - Ⓑ The ridgelines take them straight to the top.
    - ● There are no trails for hikers to take.
    - Ⓓ The ridgelines provide more shade.

**Benchmark 1**

# Benchmark 1 Answer Sheets

Benchmark 1

## Vocabulary

**Read each item. Fill in the bubble for the answer you think is correct.**

1. Rejoin means
   - (A) not join.
   - **(B) join again.**
   - (C) join many times.
   - (D) want to join.

2. Paid is the base word in prepaid. Prepaid means
   - **(A) paid ahead of time.**
   - (B) not paid.
   - (C) paid in half.
   - (D) wanting to pay.

3. Dictionary means
   - (A) a group of scientists.
   - (B) a book of number puzzles.
   - (C) a collection of stories.
   - **(D) a book of word meanings.**

4. What word means about the same as feud?
   - (A) game
   - **(B) fight**
   - (C) song
   - (D) peace

5. What word means about the same as instruct?
   - (A) forgive
   - (B) convince
   - (C) trick
   - **(D) teach**

GO ON

10 • Level 5 Benchmark Assessment • Benchmark 1

**Benchmark 1**

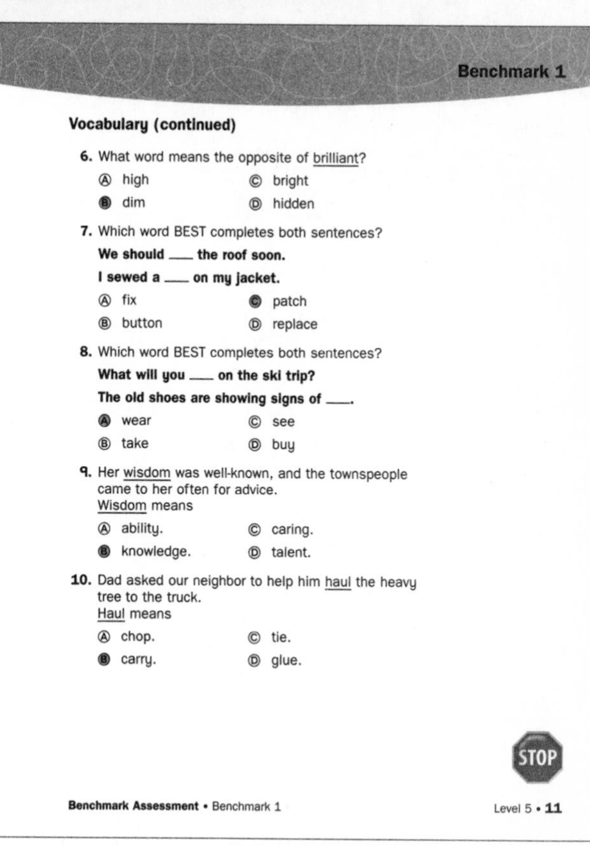

Benchmark 1

### Vocabulary (continued)

6. What word means the opposite of brilliant?
   - (A) high
   - **(B) dim**
   - (C) bright
   - (D) hidden

7. Which word BEST completes both sentences?
   **We should ___ the roof soon.**
   **I sewed a ___ on my jacket.**
   - (A) fix
   - (B) button
   - **(C) patch**
   - (D) replace

8. Which word BEST completes both sentences?
   **What will you ___ on the ski trip?**
   **The old shoes are showing signs of ___.**
   - **(A) wear**
   - (B) take
   - (C) see
   - (D) buy

9. Her wisdom was well-known, and the townspeople came to her often for advice.
   Wisdom means
   - (A) ability.
   - **(B) knowledge.**
   - (C) caring.
   - (D) talent.

10. Dad asked our neighbor to help him haul the heavy tree to the truck.
    Haul means
    - (A) chop.
    - **(B) carry.**
    - (C) tie.
    - (D) glue.

STOP

Benchmark Assessment • Benchmark 1 Level 5 • 11

**Benchmark 1**

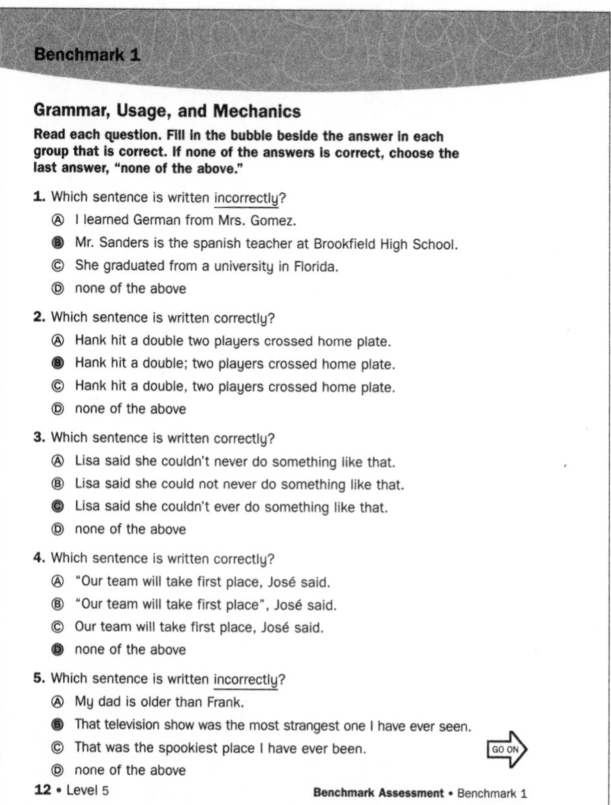

Benchmark 1

## Grammar, Usage, and Mechanics

**Read each question. Fill in the bubble beside the answer in each group that is correct. If none of the answers is correct, choose the last answer, "none of the above."**

1. Which sentence is written incorrectly?
   - (A) I learned German from Mrs. Gomez.
   - **(B) Mr. Sanders is the spanish teacher at Brookfield High School.**
   - (C) She graduated from a university in Florida.
   - (D) none of the above

2. Which sentence is written correctly?
   - (A) Hank hit a double two players crossed home plate.
   - **(B) Hank hit a double; two players crossed home plate.**
   - (C) Hank hit a double, two players crossed home plate.
   - (D) none of the above

3. Which sentence is written correctly?
   - (A) Lisa said she couldn't never do something like that.
   - (B) Lisa said she could not never do something like that.
   - **(C) Lisa said she couldn't ever do something like that.**
   - (D) none of the above

4. Which sentence is written correctly?
   - (A) "Our team will take first place, José said.
   - (B) "Our team will take first place", José said.
   - (C) Our team will take first place, José said.
   - **(D) none of the above**

5. Which sentence is written incorrectly?
   - (A) My dad is older than Frank.
   - **(B) That television show was the most strangest one I have ever seen.**
   - (C) That was the spookiest place I have ever been.
   - (D) none of the above

GO ON

12 • Level 5 Benchmark Assessment • Benchmark 1

**Benchmark 1**

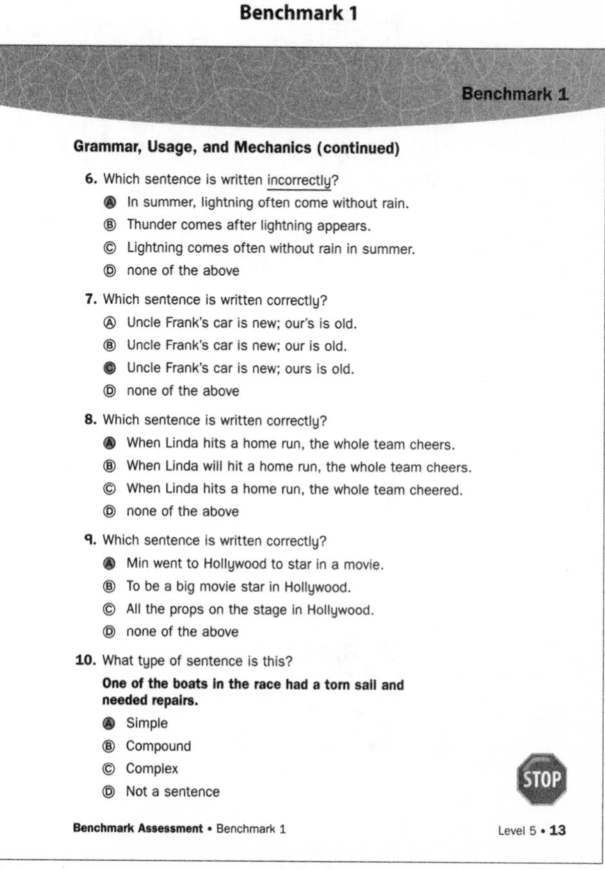

Benchmark 1

### Grammar, Usage, and Mechanics (continued)

6. Which sentence is written incorrectly?
   - **(A) In summer, lightning often come without rain.**
   - (B) Thunder comes after lightning appears.
   - (C) Lightning comes often without rain in summer.
   - (D) none of the above

7. Which sentence is written correctly?
   - (A) Uncle Frank's car is new; our's is old.
   - (B) Uncle Frank's car is new; our is old.
   - **(C) Uncle Frank's car is new; ours is old.**
   - (D) none of the above

8. Which sentence is written correctly?
   - **(A) When Linda hits a home run, the whole team cheers.**
   - (B) When Linda will hit a home run, the whole team cheers.
   - (C) When Linda hits a home run, the whole team cheered.
   - (D) none of the above

9. Which sentence is written correctly?
   - **(A) Min went to Hollywood to star in a movie.**
   - (B) To be a big movie star in Hollywood.
   - (C) All the props on the stage in Hollywood.
   - (D) none of the above

10. What type of sentence is this?
    **One of the boats in the race had a torn sail and needed repairs.**
    - **(A) Simple**
    - (B) Compound
    - (C) Complex
    - (D) Not a sentence

STOP

Benchmark Assessment • Benchmark 1 Level 5 • 13

**Benchmark 1**

# Benchmark 1 Answer Sheets

Benchmark 1

## Spelling

**Read each group of words. Only one of the words is spelled correctly. Fill in the bubble under the word that is spelled correctly.**

| | | | | |
|---|---|---|---|---|
| 1. | regular<br>● | reglar<br>Ⓑ | relugar<br>Ⓒ | regulir<br>Ⓓ |
| 2. | chepp<br>Ⓐ | cheap<br>● | chaep<br>Ⓒ | chepe<br>Ⓓ |
| 3. | suvrey<br>Ⓐ | survay<br>Ⓑ | survey<br>● | surviy<br>Ⓓ |
| 4. | seam<br>● | saem<br>Ⓑ | sem<br>Ⓒ | seemm<br>Ⓓ |
| 5. | cieling<br>Ⓐ | ceilin<br>Ⓑ | ceilinng<br>Ⓒ | ceiling<br>● |

GO ON

14 • Level 5 Benchmark Assessment • Benchmark 1

Benchmark 1

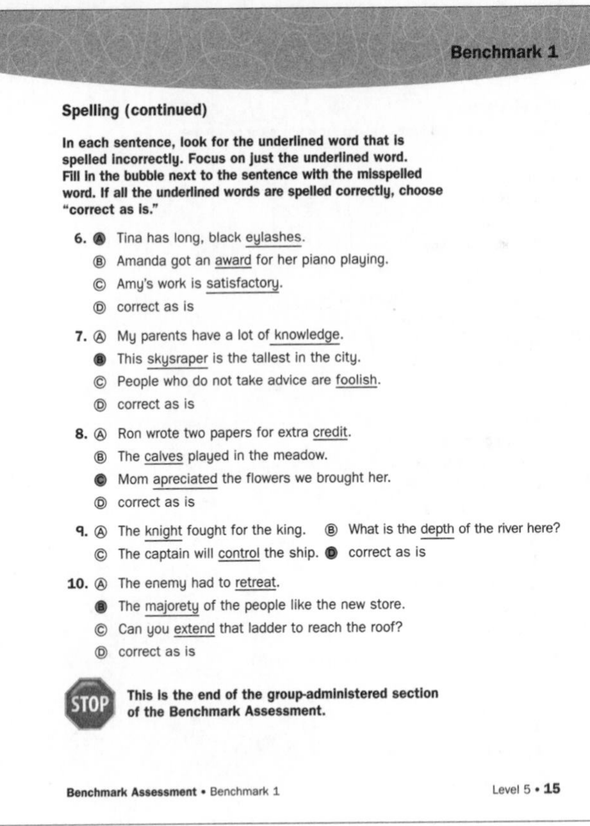

Benchmark 1

### Spelling (continued)

**In each sentence, look for the underlined word that is spelled incorrectly. Focus on just the underlined word. Fill in the bubble next to the sentence with the misspelled word. If all the underlined words are spelled correctly, choose "correct as is."**

6. ● Tina has long, black eylashes.
   Ⓑ Amanda got an award for her piano playing.
   Ⓒ Amy's work is satisfactory.
   Ⓓ correct as is
7. Ⓐ My parents have a lot of knowledge.
   ● This skysraper is the tallest in the city.
   Ⓒ People who do not take advice are foolish.
   Ⓓ correct as is
8. Ⓐ Ron wrote two papers for extra credit.
   Ⓑ The calves played in the meadow.
   ● Mom apreciated the flowers we brought her.
   Ⓓ correct as is
9. Ⓐ The knight fought for the king. Ⓑ What is the depth of the river here?
   Ⓒ The captain will control the ship. ● correct as is
10. Ⓐ The enemy had to retreat.
    ● The majorety of the people like the new store.
    Ⓒ Can you extend that ladder to reach the roof?
    Ⓓ correct as is

STOP **This is the end of the group-administered section of the Benchmark Assessment.**

Benchmark Assessment • Benchmark 1 Level 5 • 15

Benchmark 1

Benchmark 1

Name ____________ Date ________ Score ________

### Fluency MAZE Assessment

The world's oceans are filled with shipwrecks. Most of them lay hidden and **[yesterday / permission / forgotten]**. When one is found, it is a **[zip / ace / big]** deal. Historians and explorers can study **[wrong / these / blank]** shipwrecks to find out about past **[whether / cultures / accident]**.

One such shipwreck was found in 2003 **[in / of / am]** the Black Sea. The ship sank **[more / can't / dust]** than two thousand years ago. This **[ash / sea / was]** the time when the ancient Greeks **[house / lived / blame]**. Explorers hoped to find out more **[trust / about / quote]** the Greek civilization from the objects **[part / sure / they]** found in the wreck.

One thing **[they / mind / sews]** found in the shipwreck was a **[sing / such / pile]** of huge clay jars. The Greeks **[bowl / used / pass]** these jars to pack and transport **[cot / all / gel]** kinds of things. The historians wondered **[what / band / case]** kind of things had been carried **[ox / in / of]** these jars.

The answer to that **[question / convince / material]** became the real "treasure" of this **[fortunate / conclude / shipwreck]**. When the jars were first studied, **[break / fish / quote]** bones were found inside. Fish bones are **[problem / teacher / usually]** not very interesting. But this information **[era / was / fun]** very helpful to the explorers and **[discrimination / historians / considerations]**. It helped them to understand the **[types / upper / shout]** of foods ancient Greeks ate. The **[sale / thin / fish]** were probably going to feed hungry Greek **[soldiers / backfire / valuable]**.

The oceans are still filled with **[tournament / reputation / shipwrecks]** waiting to be found. Some of **[sill / talk / them]** hold amazing treasure. Others will give **[information / surrender / responsible]** about the lives of people who **[boost / lived / storm]** long ago.

18 • Level 5 Benchmark Assessment • Benchmark 1

Benchmark 1

**Comprehension (continued)**

1. This story is mostly about
   - Ⓐ a boy who helps a neighbor with weeding.
   - ● a boy who thinks up a plan to solve a problem.
   - Ⓒ a boy who helps his sister with homework.
   - Ⓓ a boy who is frustrated with his sister.
2. Nate told Allan he could not play basketball after school because he
   - Ⓐ was playing video games.
   - Ⓑ had to weed the yard.
   - ● had to watch Kayla.
   - Ⓓ wanted to do homework.
3. Why did Nate watch Kayla after school every day?
   - Ⓐ He needed the extra money.
   - Ⓑ Mrs. Young could not babysit her.
   - Ⓒ Kayla needed help with homework.
   - ● He felt it was his responsibility.
4. Nate was impatient with Kayla because
   - ● he did not want his reading interrupted.
   - Ⓑ she would not get her homework done.
   - Ⓒ he had to wait a long time for her bus.
   - Ⓓ she did not understand her homework.
5. Kayla made Nate smile when she said
   - Ⓐ that she would play basketball with him.
   - ● that he was a great teacher.
   - Ⓒ that she had finished all her homework.
   - Ⓓ that he was very good at basketball.

GO ON



Benchmark 2



**Comprehension (continued)**

6. What did Nate say was making him frustrated?
   - Ⓐ having to help Kayla with her homework every day
   - Ⓑ not doing well when he played basketball
   - ● watching Kayla when he wanted to play with friends
   - Ⓓ not being able to get to the game
7. What idea did Nate have to solve his problem?
   - Ⓐ He closed the door to keep Kayla out.
   - ● He asked Mrs. Young to babysit Kayla.
   - Ⓒ He had Mrs. Young meet Kayla's bus.
   - Ⓓ He asked his mom for more money.
8. In exchange for Mrs. Young's babysitting services
   - Ⓐ Nate's mom would pay her later.
   - Ⓑ Kayla would help around the house.
   - Ⓒ Mom would drive her to the store.
   - ● Nate agreed to weed her garden.
9. From this story, you can tell that Nate
   - ● cares about his younger sister.
   - Ⓑ is not very good at math homework.
   - Ⓒ does not have very many friends.
   - Ⓓ had never worked in a garden before.
10. Why does Nate's mom ask him to wait a few more months?
    - Ⓐ to give her time to change jobs
    - Ⓑ to give her time to quit her job
    - Ⓒ to give her time to find a sitter
    - ● to give her time to improve the situation

GO ON



Benchmark 2



**Comprehension (continued)**

1. This story is mostly about
   - Ⓐ how to get a job in the patent office.
   - Ⓑ the best way to get inventions patented.
   - Ⓒ ways to prevent cars from polluting air.
   - ● one person's unusual inventions.
2. Which of these is NOT a reason why a patent would be useful?
   - Ⓐ It lets people know who made something.
   - ● It will let an inventor keep an idea secret.
   - Ⓒ It prevents others from stealing an idea.
   - Ⓓ A patent owner will get paid if the invention is used.
3. How did Arthur Pedrick know how to apply for a patent?
   - Ⓐ His patent lawyer explained it to him.
   - ● He had worked in the patent office.
   - Ⓒ He watched other inventors at work.
   - Ⓓ He read information about patents.
4. Pedrick planned to get water to the deserts by
   - Ⓐ transferring it from the ocean.
   - Ⓑ trucking it in barrels.
   - Ⓒ making irrigation ditches.
   - ● sending snowballs through pipelines.
5. Pedrick must have known something about science because
   - ● he figured the Earth's rotation into one of his inventions.
   - Ⓑ he liked cars and transportation.
   - Ⓒ he wanted to lower air pollution.
   - Ⓓ he applied for patents.

GO ON



Benchmark 2



**Comprehension (continued)**

6. How was Pedrick's car different from a horse and buggy?
   - ● The horse pushed instead of pulled the car.
   - Ⓑ The car pushed the horse instead of pulling it.
   - Ⓒ The horse could pull the car faster than a buggy.
   - Ⓓ The car used several horses instead of just one.
7. One big disadvantage of Pedrick's car plan is
   - ● people who use it must own horses.
   - Ⓑ it would be hard on the environment.
   - Ⓒ everyone would need to buy a new car.
   - Ⓓ most people would speed on highways.
8. How did pushing on the gas pedal move the horse?
   - Ⓐ It gave the horse a shock.
   - Ⓑ The car pushed the horse ahead.
   - ● It moved the feedbox forward.
   - Ⓓ The pedal turned the wheels.
9. From the last paragraph, you can figure out that a horse's halter is something that
   - Ⓐ protects a horse's feet.
   - Ⓑ feeds a horse.
   - ● causes a horse to stop.
   - Ⓓ makes a horse stronger.
10. From this selection, you can tell that Arthur Pedrick
    - Ⓐ had no idea how to patent his inventions.
    - ● probably had a good sense of humor.
    - Ⓒ did not know much about Earth's rotation.
    - Ⓓ was not a very creative person.

STOP



Benchmark 2

# Benchmark 2 Answer Sheets



## Vocabulary

**Read each item. Fill in the bubble for the answer you think is correct.**

1. Motionless means
   - Ⓐ rolling.
   - Ⓑ melted.
   - ● still.
   - Ⓓ falling.
2. Skill is the base word in unskilled. Unskilled means
   - ● without skills.
   - Ⓑ highly skilled.
   - Ⓒ learning a skill.
   - Ⓓ sharing skills.
3. Vision means
   - Ⓐ the ability to taste.
   - Ⓑ the ability to touch.
   - Ⓒ the ability to hear.
   - ● the ability to see.
4. What word means about the same as delicate?
   - Ⓐ pretty
   - Ⓑ hardy
   - ● fragile
   - Ⓓ damaged
5. What word means about the same as proper?
   - ● correct
   - Ⓑ heaviest
   - Ⓒ expensive
   - Ⓓ wrong

GO ON



Benchmark 2



## Vocabulary (continued)

6. What word means the opposite of victory?
   - Ⓐ win
   - Ⓒ talent
   - Ⓑ tradition
   - ● loss
7. Which word BEST completes both sentences?
   **They will ___ next week.**
   **The ___ on this table is beautiful.**
   - Ⓐ arrive
   - Ⓒ run
   - Ⓑ setting
   - ● finish
8. Which word BEST completes both sentences?
   **Doug did not ___ the cold weather.**
   **Tell us if you change your ___.**
   - Ⓐ enjoy
   - Ⓒ dislike
   - Ⓑ decision
   - ● mind
9. The students in the school will attend a special meeting. Attend means
   - Ⓐ set up.
   - ● go to.
   - Ⓑ order.
   - Ⓓ enjoy.
10. The injured player missed a few games. Injured means
    - Ⓐ good.
    - Ⓒ missing.
    - Ⓑ late.
    - ● hurt.

STOP



Benchmark 2



## Grammar, Usage, and Mechanics

**Read each question. Fill in the bubble beside the answer in each group that is correct. If none of the answers is correct, choose the last answer, "none of the above."**

1. Which sentence is written correctly?
   - ● Paintings by Degas will be at Penn Art Museum on Tuesday, March 9.
   - Ⓑ Paintings by Degas will be at Penn Art Museum on tuesday, March 9.
   - Ⓒ Paintings by Degas will be at Penn art museum on Tuesday, March 9.
   - Ⓓ none of the above
2. Which sentence is written incorrectly?
   - ● Five students won gold medals Raul, Lia, Yin, Aaron, and Latoya.
   - Ⓑ The medals were actually made from these metals: gold, brass, and bronze.
   - Ⓒ They all had one goal: finish in first place.
   - Ⓓ none of the above
3. Which sentence is written correctly?
   - Ⓐ Our family never does nothing during vacations.
   - ● Our family never does anything during vacations.
   - Ⓒ Our family doesn't never do anything during vacations.
   - Ⓓ none of the above
4. Which sentence is written correctly?
   - Ⓐ Pete asked, "Which gift is for Grandma's birthday"?
   - Ⓑ Pete asked, Which gift is for Grandma's birthday?"
   - ● Pete asked, "Which gift is for Grandma's birthday?"
   - Ⓓ none of the above
5. Which sentence is written correctly?
   - ● Do you think Mark runs more quickly than Adam?
   - Ⓑ Do you think Mark runs more quicklier than Adam?
   - Ⓒ Do you think Mark runs the most quickly than Adam?
   - Ⓓ none of the above

GO ON



Benchmark 2



## Grammar, Usage, and Mechanics (continued)

6. Which sentence is written incorrectly?
   - Ⓐ The high school and middle school were working on a play.
   - ● Julie and Ari loves being on stage in school plays.
   - Ⓒ In their play, someone always yells from the side.
   - Ⓓ none of the above
7. Which sentence is written correctly?
   - Ⓐ Maren and him are going to the movies next week.
   - Ⓑ Maren and his are going to the movies next week.
   - Ⓒ Him and Maren are going to the movies next week.
   - ● none of the above
8. Which sentence is written correctly?
   - Ⓐ When the bell rings, school was over for the day.
   - Ⓑ When the bell rang, school is over for the day.
   - Ⓒ When the bell rang, school will be over for the day.
   - ● none of the above
9. Which sentence is written correctly?
   - Ⓐ Food for the animals in the zoo.
   - Ⓑ All the cages of the hungry animals in the Parkline Zoo.
   - ● The hungry zebras, tigers, monkeys, and rhinos ate quickly.
   - Ⓓ none of the above
10. What type of sentence is this?
    **One hundred large peacocks with their tails fanned out.**
    - Ⓐ Simple
    - Ⓑ Compound
    - Ⓒ Complex
    - ● Not a sentence

STOP



Benchmark 2

Benchmark 2

## Spelling

**Read each group of words. Only one of the words is spelled correctly. Fill in the bubble under the word that is spelled correctly.**

| | | | | |
|---|---|---|---|---|
| 1. | sefaty Ⓐ | saftey Ⓑ | saffety Ⓒ | safety ● |
| 2. | additional ● | aditional Ⓑ | aditionnal Ⓒ | additionel Ⓓ |
| 3. | presecne Ⓐ | presence ● | persence Ⓒ | presense Ⓓ |
| 4. | farbric Ⓐ | febric Ⓑ | fabrick Ⓒ | fabric ● |
| 5. | fondation Ⓐ | foudation Ⓑ | foundation ● | fuondasion Ⓓ |

GO ON

32 • Level 5 Benchmark Assessment • Benchmark 2

Benchmark 2

Benchmark 2

## Spelling (continued)

**In each sentence, look for the underlined word that is spelled incorrectly. Focus on just the underlined word. Fill in the bubble next to the sentence with the misspelled word. If all the underlined words are spelled correctly, choose "correct as is."**

6. ● The casheir gave us the wrong change.
   Ⓑ Monday is laundry day at our house.
   Ⓒ Sometimes Leah is impatient with her brother.
   Ⓓ correct as is
7. Ⓐ Avery learned a new chord on his guitar.
   Ⓑ The queen chose a jewel for her crown.
   ● The hikers found pieces of pertrified wood.
   Ⓓ correct as is
8. Ⓐ Liam needed his parents' approval to join.
   Ⓑ My little sister can be a real nuisance!
   ● Semir's brother is a junour in high school.
   Ⓓ correct as is
9. Ⓐ Pedro likes to plunge right into the water.
   ● The friends made up after their quarrell.
   Ⓒ The hotel provides breakfast every morning.
   Ⓓ correct as is
10. Ⓐ He gave us an estimate on the house.
    Ⓑ Visitors need a passport to cross the border.
    Ⓒ Do you have something to occupy you while you wait?
    ● correct as is

**This is the end of the group-administered section of the Benchmark Assessment.**

Benchmark Assessment • Benchmark 2 Level 5 • 33

Benchmark 2

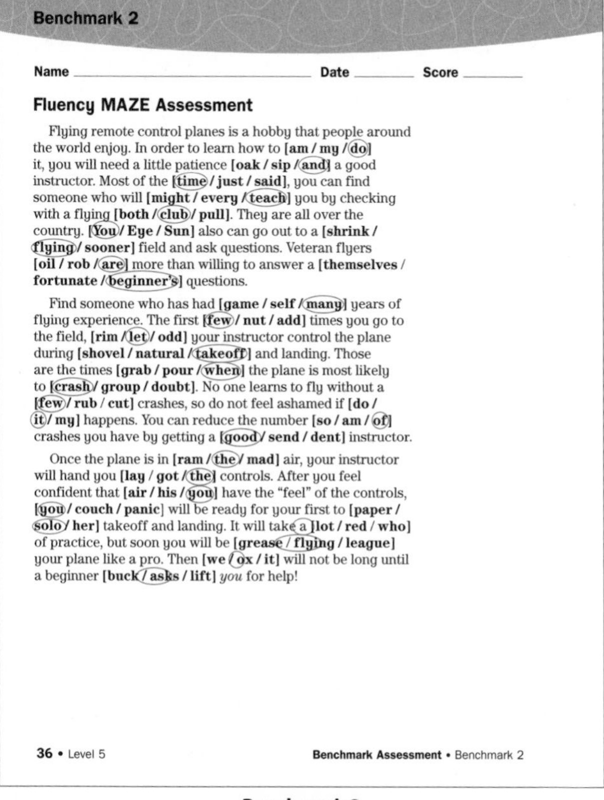
Benchmark 2

Name ______________ Date ________ Score ________

## Fluency MAZE Assessment

Flying remote control planes is a hobby that people around the world enjoy. In order to learn how to **[am / my / do]** it, you will need a little patience **[oak / sip / and]** a good instructor. Most of the **[time / just / said]**, you can find someone who will **[might / every / teach]** you by checking with a flying **[both / club / pull]**. They are all over the country. **[You / Eye / Sun]** also can go out to a **[shrink / flying / sooner]** field and ask questions. Veteran flyers **[oil / rob / are]** more than willing to answer a **[themselves / fortunate / beginner's]** questions.

Find someone who has had **[game / self / many]** years of flying experience. The first **[few / nut / add]** times you go to the field, **[rim / let / odd]** your instructor control the plane during **[shovel / natural / takeoff]** and landing. Those are the times **[grab / pour / when]** the plane is most likely to **[crash / group / doubt]**. No one learns to fly without a **[few / rub / cut]** crashes, so do not feel ashamed if **[do / it / my]** happens. You can reduce the number **[so / am / of]** crashes you have by getting a **[good / send / dent]** instructor.

Once the plane is in **[ram / the / mad]** air, your instructor will hand you **[lay / got / the]** controls. After you feel confident that **[air / his / you]** have the "feel" of the controls, **[you / couch / panic]** will be ready for your first to **[paper / solo / her]** takeoff and landing. It will take a **[lot / red / who]** of practice, but soon you will be **[grease / flying / league]** your plane like a pro. Then **[we / ox / it]** will not be long until a beginner **[buck / asks / lift]** *you* for help!

36 • Level 5 Benchmark Assessment • Benchmark 2

Benchmark 2

# Benchmark 3 Answer Sheets

Benchmark 3

**Comprehension (continued)**

1. This story is mostly about
   - Ⓐ a grandfather repairing old-fashioned tools.
   - Ⓑ how to wet harvest cranberries.
   - **Ⓒ a girl picking cranberries with her grandfather.**
   - Ⓓ why dry harvesting is better than wet harvesting.
2. What was the earliest tool people used for picking cranberries?
   - Ⓐ the wooden comb
   - Ⓑ the metal snap scoop
   - Ⓒ a harvesting machine
   - **Ⓓ their fingers**
3. Why do people dry harvest cranberries?
   - Ⓐ It is easier to do than wet harvesting.
   - Ⓑ The growing season is much shorter.
   - Ⓒ It takes much less time to dry harvest.
   - **Ⓓ They need to pick perfect berries to sell whole.**
4. What is one advantage of wet harvesting cranberries?
   - **Ⓐ Pickers do not worry about berries, so they go fast.**
   - Ⓑ The berries can be harvested much sooner.
   - Ⓒ Perfect berries are the only ones that are picked.
   - Ⓓ The berries are wet, so they do not need to be washed.
5. Why did Cheri run the dry harvesting machine?
   - Ⓐ Her parents had bought it for her.
   - Ⓑ She could run it better than Grandpa.
   - **Ⓒ Her grandfather was feeling tired.**
   - Ⓓ Grandpa could not use modern tools.

Benchmark Assessment • Benchmark 3 Level 5 • 39

**Benchmark 3**

Benchmark 3

**Comprehension (continued)**

6. What usually happens to wet harvested cranberries?
   - Ⓐ They are sold whole in bags.
   - **Ⓑ They are crushed for juice or sauce.**
   - Ⓒ They are dried to make new seeds.
   - Ⓓ They are fed to cattle and pigs.
7. Cranberry picking changed over the years in all these ways EXCEPT
   - Ⓐ motorized machines are used.
   - **Ⓑ most people now use hand tools.**
   - Ⓒ picking has gotten faster.
   - Ⓓ it has become much easier.
8. From this story, you can tell that Cheri
   - **Ⓐ enjoys being with her grandpa.**
   - Ⓑ does not know much about old tools.
   - Ⓒ has used the harvesting machine many times.
   - Ⓓ picks cranberries very quickly.
9. Which of the following would probably use a wet harvesting machine?
   - Ⓐ a small farm
   - Ⓑ an individual berry picker
   - **Ⓒ a company that manufactures cranberry sauce**
   - Ⓓ a company that sells whole berries
10. Most pickers do seventy-five barrels a day. Why did Cheri think sixty-seven was good?
    - **Ⓐ She is still learning.**
    - Ⓑ Wet harvesting is slower.
    - Ⓒ They have a small farm.
    - Ⓓ They used old tools.

GO ON

40 • Level 5 Benchmark Assessment • Benchmark 3

**Benchmark 3**

Benchmark 3

**Comprehension (continued)**

1. This story is mostly about
   - **Ⓐ the correct way to use and display the American flag.**
   - Ⓑ how the colonies decided on a design for the flag.
   - Ⓒ why an American flag is lowered to half-staff.
   - Ⓓ when an American flag is usually flown.
2. The first flag law said the American flag would have
   - Ⓐ stars in a straight line on a dark blue background.
   - Ⓑ six red stripes and seven white stripes.
   - Ⓒ stars in a circle above seven red and white stripes.
   - **Ⓓ red and white stripes and stars on a blue background.**
3. How has the American flag changed over the years?
   - Ⓐ It has gotten much larger every year.
   - **Ⓑ It now has fifty stars instead of thirteen.**
   - Ⓒ It has a different background color.
   - Ⓓ It now has seven red and white stripes.
4. The main reason people treat the flag with respect is
   - **Ⓐ they see it as a symbol for the country.**
   - Ⓑ they are copying what other people do.
   - Ⓒ they are impressed by how old the flag is.
   - Ⓓ they were taught to do it in school.
5. How should a flag be raised to the top of a pole?
   - Ⓐ It should be raised slowly after sunrise.
   - Ⓑ It should be raised quickly every evening.
   - **Ⓒ It should be raised quickly after sunrise.**
   - Ⓓ It should be raised slowly in the morning.

Benchmark Assessment • Benchmark 3 Level 5 • 43

**Benchmark 3**

Benchmark 3

**Comprehension (continued)**

6. The American flag should be flown
   - Ⓐ every day in rain or sun.
   - **Ⓑ on the patriotic holidays.**
   - Ⓒ only on Memorial Day.
   - Ⓓ only over schools and offices.
7. The reason the American flag is flown at half-staff is
   - Ⓐ to get people's attention.
   - **Ⓑ to show great sadness.**
   - Ⓒ to let it fly more freely.
   - Ⓓ to honor most holidays.
8. All of these are rules for using the flag EXCEPT
   - Ⓐ never carry it flat or let it touch the ground.
   - Ⓑ do not hang it with the stars down.
   - Ⓒ only fly waterproof flags in the rain.
   - **Ⓓ fly it at half-staff on weekends.**
9. From this selection you can tell that the flag
   - **Ⓐ is very important to many Americans.**
   - Ⓑ has not changed much over the years.
   - Ⓒ is not thought about much.
   - Ⓓ is rarely flown on American holidays.
10. Why would a flag be important to a new country?
    - Ⓐ to show that it is powerful
    - Ⓑ to protect it from enemies
    - **Ⓒ to show that it is independent**
    - Ⓓ to explain its struggles

STOP

44 • Level 5 Benchmark Assessment • Benchmark 3

**Benchmark 3**

### Vocabulary

**Read each item. Fill in the bubble for the answer you think is correct.**

1. Convention means
   - Ⓐ quarrel.
   - Ⓑ meeting.
   - Ⓒ purchase.
   - Ⓓ surprise.
2. Close is the base word in enclose. Enclose means
   - Ⓐ open widely.
   - Ⓑ surround.
   - Ⓒ meet with.
   - Ⓓ escape from.
3. Inspire means
   - Ⓐ get people to do better.
   - Ⓑ make people tired.
   - Ⓒ find new friends.
   - Ⓓ do something without thinking.
4. What word means about the same as peculiar?
   - Ⓐ strange
   - Ⓑ pretty
   - Ⓒ normal
   - Ⓓ bright
5. What word means about the same as frequently?
   - Ⓐ happily
   - Ⓑ rarely
   - Ⓒ plugged
   - Ⓓ often

GO ON







### Vocabulary (continued)

6. What word means the opposite of nervous?
   - Ⓐ calm
   - Ⓑ tired
   - Ⓒ anxious
   - Ⓓ proud
7. What word BEST completes both sentences?
   **The ___ was locked at five o'clock.**
   **Sandy was ___ at second base.**
   - Ⓐ safe
   - Ⓑ door
   - Ⓒ out
   - Ⓓ store
8. What word BEST completes both sentences?
   **An army ___ is near our town.**
   **A large ___ held up the roof.**
   - Ⓐ post
   - Ⓑ fort
   - Ⓒ log
   - Ⓓ base
9. Jessie was exhausted after running the ten-mile race. Exhausted means
   - Ⓐ dizzy.
   - Ⓑ very happy.
   - Ⓒ very tired.
   - Ⓓ bruised.
10. The teacher will demonstrate the experiment before the class goes to the lab. Demonstrate means
    - Ⓐ begin.
    - Ⓑ show.
    - Ⓒ fix.
    - Ⓓ build.

STOP







### Grammar, Usage, and Mechanics

**Read each question. Fill in the bubble beside the answer in each group that is correct. If none of the answers is correct, choose the last answer, "none of the above."**

1. Which sentence is written correctly?
   - Ⓐ The yacht *Marlin* won first prize in the Bay city race last Thursday.
   - Ⓑ The yacht *Marlin* won First prize in the Bay City race last Thursday.
   - Ⓒ The yacht *Marlin* won first prize in the Bay City race last Thursday.
   - Ⓓ none of the above
2. Which sentence is written correctly?
   - Ⓐ Trouble comes in threes: I lost my glove, my bat, and my ball.
   - Ⓑ Trouble comes in threes I lost my glove, my bat, and my ball.
   - Ⓒ Trouble comes in threes, I lost my glove, my bat, and my ball.
   - Ⓓ none of the above
3. Which sentence is written incorrectly?
   - Ⓐ I am not leaving these things on the table.
   - Ⓑ Do not touch none of those things while I am gone.
   - Ⓒ No one touched anything on my desk.
   - Ⓓ none of the above
4. Which sentence is written correctly?
   - Ⓐ "wait for me at the corner," Dad told my brother.
   - Ⓑ "Wait for me at the corner", Dad told my brother.
   - Ⓒ "Wait for me at the corner," Dad told my brother.
   - Ⓓ none of the above
5. Which sentence is written correctly?
   - Ⓐ Do you think a pig is more intelligenter than a dog?
   - Ⓑ Do you think a pig is more intelligent than a dog?
   - Ⓒ Do you think a pig is most intelligent than a dog?
   - Ⓓ none of the above

GO ON







### Grammar, Usage, and Mechanics (continued)

6. Which sentence is written correctly?
   - Ⓐ The cows in the meadow were not eating the grass.
   - Ⓑ The cows in the meadow was not eating the grass.
   - Ⓒ In the meadow the cows was not eating the grass.
   - Ⓓ none of the above
7. Which sentence is written correctly?
   - Ⓐ My friend's costume was scary, but my's was funny.
   - Ⓑ My friend's costume was scary, but mine's was funny.
   - Ⓒ My friend's costume was scary, but mine was funny.
   - Ⓓ none of the above
8. Which sentence is written incorrectly?
   - Ⓐ When the airplane landed, the ground crew began its job.
   - Ⓑ They opened the hatch and unloaded fifty suitcases.
   - Ⓒ Part of the crew took the luggage while the rest serviced the plane.
   - Ⓓ none of the above
9. Which sentence is written correctly?
   - Ⓐ The canoe had to be carried around the rapids.
   - Ⓑ Rapids that are dangerous and canoes that can tip over.
   - Ⓒ The most dangerous rapids on the Colorado River.
   - Ⓓ none of the above
10. What type of sentence is this?
    **Five workers lifted the heavy beam, and two others nailed it up.**
    - Ⓐ Simple
    - Ⓑ Compound
    - Ⓒ Complex
    - Ⓓ Not a sentence

STOP

# Benchmark 3 Answer Sheets

Benchmark 3

## Spelling

**Read each group of words. Only one of the words is spelled correctly. Fill in the bubble under the word that is spelled correctly.**

| | | | | |
|---|---|---|---|---|
| **1.** | eraser | erasur | erraser | eracer |
| | ● | Ⓑ | Ⓒ | Ⓓ |
| **2.** | wierd | weerd | weird | werid |
| | Ⓐ | Ⓑ | ● | Ⓓ |
| **3.** | sholarship | scholarship | scholership | scholasrhip |
| | Ⓐ | ● | Ⓒ | Ⓓ |
| **4.** | fayde | fede | faid | fade |
| | Ⓐ | Ⓑ | Ⓒ | ● |
| **5.** | terribly | teribly | turibly | terribley |
| | ● | Ⓑ | Ⓒ | Ⓓ |

GO ON



Benchmark 3

Benchmark 3

## Spelling (continued)

**In each sentence, look for the underlined word that is spelled incorrectly. Focus on just the underlined word. Fill in the bubble next to the sentence with the misspelled word. If all the underlined words are spelled correctly, choose "correct as is."**

**6.** Ⓐ How much damage did the accident cause?
Ⓑ Winning the game was a real triumph.
Ⓒ Ellen hunches down before she races.
● correct as is

**7.** Ⓐ The cinema has the new movie.
● What is the name of the cereal manufactarer?
Ⓒ Peg needed three egg yolks for the cake.
Ⓓ correct as is

**8.** ● My brother goes to the elementery school.
Ⓑ Please greet the visitors when they arrive.
Ⓒ The recipe said to soften the butter.
Ⓓ correct as is

**9.** Ⓐ The willow tree had long, slender branches.
Ⓑ We always buy school supplies in the summer.
● What will you weer to the dance?
Ⓓ correct as is

**10.** Ⓐ My aunt's car is lime green.
Ⓑ The farmer used a tractor to plow.
Ⓒ A helmet will prevent a head injury.
● correct as is

**This is the end of the group-administered section of the Benchmark Assessment.**



Benchmark 3

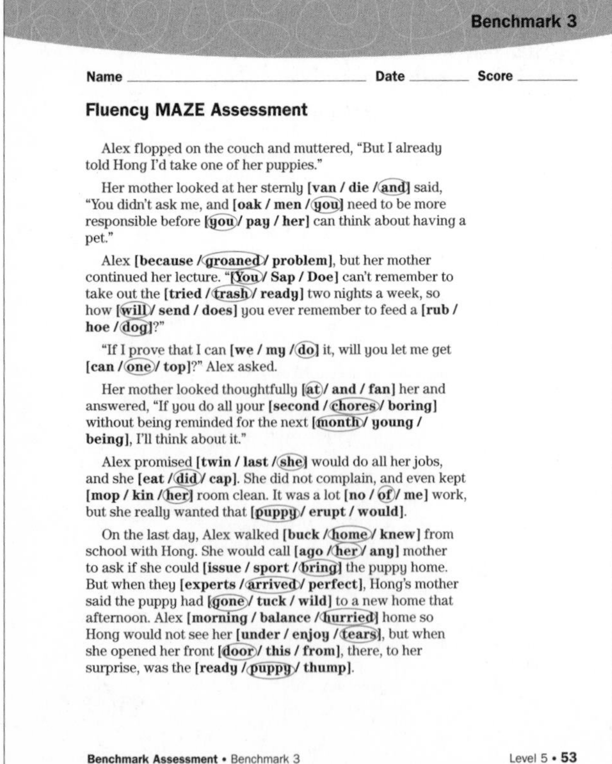

Benchmark 3

**Name** ______________ **Date** ________ **Score** ________

## Fluency MAZE Assessment

Alex flopped on the couch and muttered, "But I already told Hong I'd take one of her puppies."

Her mother looked at her sternly **[van / die / and]** said, "You didn't ask me, and **[oak / men / you]** need to be more responsible before **[you / pay / her]** can think about having a pet."

Alex **[because / groaned / problem]**, but her mother continued her lecture. "**[You / Sap / Doe]** can't remember to take out the **[tried / trash / ready]** two nights a week, so how **[will / send / does]** you ever remember to feed a **[rub / hoe / dog]**?"

"If I prove that I can **[we / my / do]** it, will you let me get **[can / one / top]**?" Alex asked.

Her mother looked thoughtfully **[at / and / fan]** her and answered, "If you do all your **[second / chores / boring]** without being reminded for the next **[month / young / being]**, I'll think about it."

Alex promised **[twin / last / she]** would do all her jobs, and she **[eat / did / cap]**. She did not complain, and even kept **[mop / kin / her]** room clean. It was a lot **[no / of / me]** work, but she really wanted that **[puppy / erupt / would]**.

On the last day, Alex walked **[buck / home / knew]** from school with Hong. She would call **[ago / her / any]** mother to ask if she could **[issue / sport / bring]** the puppy home. But when they **[experts / arrived / perfect]**, Hong's mother said the puppy had **[gone / tuck / wild]** to a new home that afternoon. Alex **[morning / balance / hurried]** home so Hong would not see her **[under / enjoy / tears]**, but when she opened her front **[door / this / from]**, there, to her surprise, was the **[ready / puppy / thump]**.



Benchmark 3

# Benchmark 4 Answer Sheets



**Comprehension (continued)**

**1.** This story is mostly about
- Ⓐ the rules of golf.
- ● a memorable golf shot.
- Ⓒ golf courses in the South.
- Ⓓ how to improve your golf game.

**2.** From what point of view is this story written?
- Ⓐ second-person
- Ⓑ third-person
- ● first-person
- Ⓓ Dad's point of view

**3.** Why do the narrator and her father fly south?
- Ⓐ to visit family
- Ⓑ to see a ball game
- Ⓒ to fish
- ● to play golf

**4.** The narrator and her dad stay at a hotel
- Ⓐ on the golf course.
- Ⓑ by the creek.
- ● near a beach.
- Ⓓ next to a pond.

**5.** How can you tell the story is set during the winter?
- ● The pond back home is frozen.
- Ⓑ People golf only in the winter.
- Ⓒ The narrator goes to the beach.
- Ⓓ The narrator's dad has a rental car.

GO ON



Benchmark 4



**Comprehension (continued)**

**6.** Where is the flag on the golf course?
- Ⓐ in the creek
- ● on the green
- Ⓒ on the tee
- Ⓓ in the woods

**7.** The first time the narrator hits the golf ball it goes
- Ⓐ onto the green.
- Ⓑ into the cup.
- ● into the creek.
- Ⓓ over the green.

**8.** How many balls does the narrator hit into the creek?
- Ⓐ 1
- Ⓑ 5
- Ⓒ 3
- ● 2

**9.** According to the story, you know that Dad
- ● got his ball on the green first.
- Ⓑ visits the same courses every year.
- Ⓒ is impatient on the golf course.
- Ⓓ is a professional golfer.

**10.** Based on what you read in the story, the narrator probably
- Ⓐ has never played golf before.
- Ⓑ has been playing golf for many years.
- Ⓒ has no interest in playing golf again.
- ● has been playing golf for a short time.

GO ON



Benchmark 4



**Comprehension (continued)**

**1.** This selection is about how
- Ⓐ women did not make good stagecoach drivers.
- Ⓑ driving a stagecoach was an easy job.
- ● a woman posed as a man and drove a stagecoach.
- Ⓓ people voted for president a long time ago.

**2.** Stagecoach drivers had to be brave for all these reasons EXCEPT
- Ⓐ they had to drive in all kinds of weather.
- Ⓑ they faced robbers and wild animals.
- Ⓒ the roads were dangerous and scary.
- ● they often fought with passengers.

**3.** Which of these is NOT a reason why roads were dangerous?
- Ⓐ They were winding and steep.
- Ⓑ There were no guardrails.
- Ⓒ Robbers often lay in wait.
- ● They went into small towns.

**4.** Charley wore a patch because
- Ⓐ he liked the way it looked.
- ● he had lost an eye in an accident.
- Ⓒ he had an eye infection.
- Ⓓ he needed a disguise.

**5.** What happened after trains came to the West?
- Ⓐ Stagecoach drivers took different routes.
- ● Stagecoaches were no longer needed.
- Ⓒ Stagecoach drivers liked to race trains.
- Ⓓ Stagecoaches moved farther north.

GO ON



Benchmark 4



**Comprehension (continued)**

**6.** Why was it unusual that Charley voted?
- ● Women were not allowed to vote.
- Ⓑ Charley did not know how to read.
- Ⓒ Men did not often vote back then.
- Ⓓ Charley showed no interest in politics.

**7.** What secret did Charley keep all his life?
- Ⓐ that he was afraid to drive
- Ⓑ that he had lost one eye
- ● that he was a woman
- Ⓓ that he had voted

**8.** From this selection, you can tell that
- Ⓐ Charley was not a very brave person.
- Ⓑ Charley had to learn to drive faster.
- Ⓒ Charley did not usually want to vote.
- ● Charley was a very determined person.

**9.** Why did Charlotte have to pretend to be someone else?
- ● to have a job women were not allowed to do
- Ⓑ to keep safe from robbers on the roads
- Ⓒ to hide out from the law
- Ⓓ to avoid people from her past

**10.** Why do you think Charley kept to himself?
- ● He did not want people to know his secret.
- Ⓑ He was shy around other people.
- Ⓒ He was embarrassed about the way his eye looked.
- Ⓓ He preferred the company of horses to people.

STOP



Benchmark 4

## Vocabulary

**Read each item. Fill in the bubble for the answer you think is correct.**

1. Independence means
   - Ⓐ requirement.
   - Ⓑ peaceful.
   - Ⓒ confusion.
   - ● freedom.
2. Serve is the base word in servant. Servant means
   - Ⓐ the way that something is served.
   - Ⓑ plates on which food is served.
   - ● someone who serves.
   - Ⓓ food that is served.
3. Nautical means
   - Ⓐ about clouds and rain.
   - ● relating to the ocean.
   - Ⓒ dealing with rocks.
   - Ⓓ involved with outer space.
4. What word means about the same as grumpy?
   - Ⓐ sick
   - Ⓑ happy
   - ● crabby
   - Ⓓ late
5. What word means about the same as concerned?
   - Ⓐ carefree
   - Ⓑ lazy
   - ● worried
   - Ⓓ quick

GO ON



Benchmark 4



## Vocabulary (continued)

6. What word means the opposite of ordinary?
   - Ⓐ typical
   - Ⓑ free
   - ● unusual
   - Ⓓ natural
7. Which word BEST completes both sentences?
   **You can earn ___ on your money.**
   **Her greatest ___ is African art.**
   - Ⓐ profits
   - Ⓑ enjoyment
   - Ⓒ payment
   - ● interest
8. Which word BEST completes both sentences?
   **The ___ is closed for the holiday.**
   **The ___ of the stream is muddy.**
   - ● bank
   - Ⓑ store
   - Ⓒ side
   - Ⓓ park
9. The compact car could not hold five passengers. Compact means
   - Ⓐ foreign.
   - Ⓑ broken.
   - Ⓒ old.
   - ● small.
10. The secretive artist will not reveal her new painting before the show opens. Reveal means
    - ● uncover.
    - Ⓑ sell.
    - Ⓒ draw.
    - Ⓓ take.

STOP



Benchmark 4

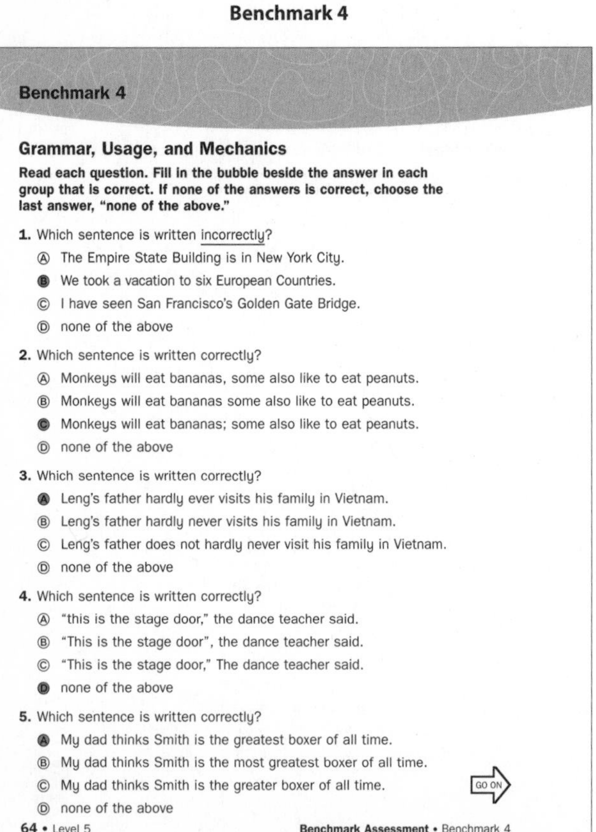



## Grammar, Usage, and Mechanics

**Read each question. Fill in the bubble beside the answer in each group that is correct. If none of the answers is correct, choose the last answer, "none of the above."**

1. Which sentence is written incorrectly?
   - Ⓐ The Empire State Building is in New York City.
   - ● We took a vacation to six European Countries.
   - Ⓒ I have seen San Francisco's Golden Gate Bridge.
   - Ⓓ none of the above
2. Which sentence is written correctly?
   - Ⓐ Monkeys will eat bananas, some also like to eat peanuts.
   - Ⓑ Monkeys will eat bananas some also like to eat peanuts.
   - ● Monkeys will eat bananas; some also like to eat peanuts.
   - Ⓓ none of the above
3. Which sentence is written correctly?
   - ● Leng's father hardly ever visits his family in Vietnam.
   - Ⓑ Leng's father hardly never visits his family in Vietnam.
   - Ⓒ Leng's father does not hardly never visit his family in Vietnam.
   - Ⓓ none of the above
4. Which sentence is written correctly?
   - Ⓐ "this is the stage door," the dance teacher said.
   - Ⓑ "This is the stage door", the dance teacher said.
   - Ⓒ "This is the stage door," The dance teacher said.
   - ● none of the above
5. Which sentence is written correctly?
   - ● My dad thinks Smith is the greatest boxer of all time.
   - Ⓑ My dad thinks Smith is the most greatest boxer of all time.
   - Ⓒ My dad thinks Smith is the greater boxer of all time.
   - Ⓓ none of the above

GO ON



Benchmark 4

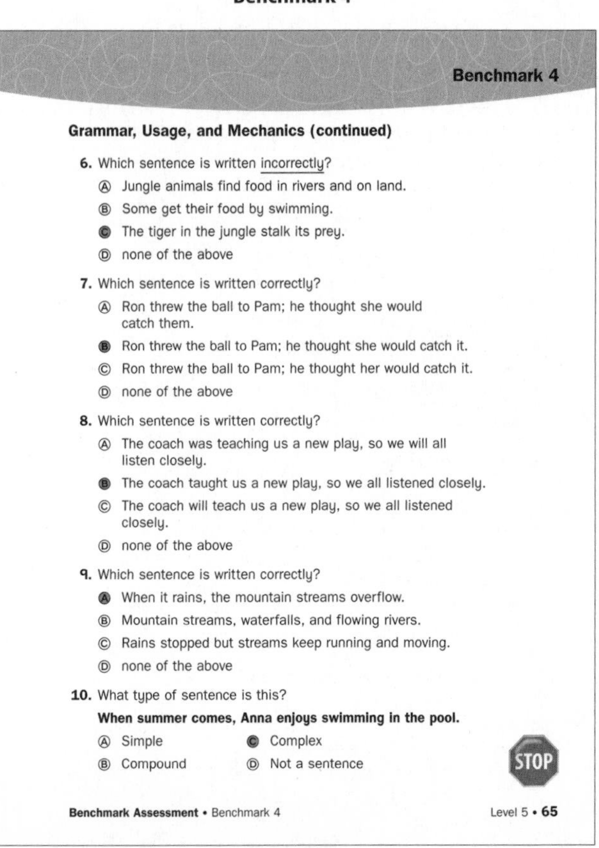



## Grammar, Usage, and Mechanics (continued)

6. Which sentence is written incorrectly?
   - Ⓐ Jungle animals find food in rivers and on land.
   - Ⓑ Some get their food by swimming.
   - ● The tiger in the jungle stalk its prey.
   - Ⓓ none of the above
7. Which sentence is written correctly?
   - Ⓐ Ron threw the ball to Pam; he thought she would catch them.
   - ● Ron threw the ball to Pam; he thought she would catch it.
   - Ⓒ Ron threw the ball to Pam; he thought her would catch it.
   - Ⓓ none of the above
8. Which sentence is written correctly?
   - Ⓐ The coach was teaching us a new play, so we will all listen closely.
   - ● The coach taught us a new play, so we all listened closely.
   - Ⓒ The coach will teach us a new play, so we all listened closely.
   - Ⓓ none of the above
9. Which sentence is written correctly?
   - ● When it rains, the mountain streams overflow.
   - Ⓑ Mountain streams, waterfalls, and flowing rivers.
   - Ⓒ Rains stopped but streams keep running and moving.
   - Ⓓ none of the above
10. What type of sentence is this?
    **When summer comes, Anna enjoys swimming in the pool.**
    - Ⓐ Simple
    - Ⓑ Compound
    - ● Complex
    - Ⓓ Not a sentence

STOP



Benchmark 4

## Spelling

**Read each group of words. Only one of the words is spelled correctly. Fill in the bubble under the word that is spelled correctly.**

| | | | | |
|---|---|---|---|---|
| **1.** | exmpt<br>Ⓐ | exemtp<br>Ⓑ | exemept<br>Ⓒ | exempt<br>● |
| **2.** | fiathful<br>Ⓐ | faithful<br>● | faithfull<br>Ⓒ | faythful<br>Ⓓ |
| **3.** | refewge<br>Ⓐ | reffugy<br>Ⓑ | refuge<br>● | refug<br>Ⓓ |
| **4.** | unbeaten<br>● | unbaeten<br>Ⓑ | unebaten<br>Ⓒ | unbeatten<br>Ⓓ |
| **5.** | wedth<br>Ⓐ | widht<br>Ⓑ | wiedth<br>Ⓒ | width<br>● |

GO ON



Benchmark 4



## Spelling (continued)

**In each sentence, look for the underlined word that is spelled incorrectly. Focus on just the underlined word. Fill in the bubble next to the sentence with the misspelled word. If all the underlined words are spelled correctly, choose "correct as is."**

**6.** Ⓐ Lily's directions were misleading.
Ⓑ No one knew what the object was.
Ⓒ My dog will bury any bone he finds.
● correct as is

**7.** Ⓐ Use arrows to indicate the correct path.
Ⓑ Tim packed a suitcase for the trip.
● That light swich does not work.
Ⓓ correct as is

**8.** Ⓐ Lora had a file for her favorite pictures.
● Henri was the only pasenger on the train.
Ⓒ In late afternoon, the tree casts a long shadow.
Ⓓ correct as is

**9.** ● Most stories have at least one herioic figure.
Ⓑ Strong winds caused the snow to drift.
Ⓒ Visitors are limited to this side of the castle.
Ⓓ correct as is

**10.** Ⓐ Can we come to an agreement?
● Our class is taking a field trip to the musuem.
Ⓒ Some animals are bred for strength.
Ⓓ correct as is

STOP **This is the end of the group-administered section of the Benchmark Assessment.**



Benchmark 4

**Name** ______________ **Date** ________ **Score** ________

## Fluency MAZE Assessment

Crop circles first made the news in the 1980s. Few people had heard of crop **[problem / circles / incline]** before then, but then the first **[dreamed / thought / circles]** were discovered in England. These circles **[so / of / it]** crushed plants appeared in the middle **[of / by / no]** fields. If humans made the circles, **[hard / says / they]** left no clues. How could they **[have / fame / care]** gotten into the field without leaving **[any / sit / are]** traces?

Right away, some people thought **[we / of / so]** aliens, believing that spaceships might have **[left / sink / idea]** the marks. Other people thought the **[recently / improve / weather]** or natural forces made them. Scientists **[wondered / footstep / daughter]** if strong winds or changes in **[out / the / ask]** soil caused the marks.

For **[homes / years / novel]**, people were not really sure. Then in 1991, **[two / are / led]** men claimed they made the circles. **[Heat / Show / They]** sneaked into the fields at night **[so / by / us]** walking between rows of crops. Using **[easier / string / should]** and a board, they flattened the **[grass / makes / songs]** into a circle. They each wore a **[cap / sip / law]** with a loop of wire over **[rip / toe / one]** eye. Looking through the loop at a **[landmark / convince / reassure]** helped them keep the circles straight.

**[Splendid / Although / Reviewed]** the men said they had made **[morning / circles / playing]**, they had not made all of them. **[Ever / Rock / Crop]** circles have been found in many **[guideline / something / countries]**. Others may have copied their idea, **[but / he's / own]** some people still wonder if humans **[colt / sons / have]** made all crop circles.



Benchmark 4

# Benchmark 5 Answer Sheets



**Comprehension (continued)**

**1.** This story is mostly about
- 🅐 a boy who wants a skateboard.
- Ⓑ how to choose a new skateboard.
- Ⓒ a girl who helps with a problem.
- Ⓓ how to do new skateboard moves.

**2.** What were Lee's friends doing while he watched?
- Ⓐ They were going to skateboarding competitions.
- Ⓑ They were checking out prices of skateboards.
- Ⓒ They were playing basketball at the park.
- 🅓 They were practicing their skateboarding moves.

**3.** In the beginning, why did Lee not have a skateboard?
- Ⓐ His mom thought they were dangerous.
- Ⓑ He did not know how to ride one.
- 🅒 He could not afford one.
- Ⓓ His friends would not let him borrow theirs.

**4.** Who told Lee about another place to shop?
- 🅐 a girl who was skateboarding past
- Ⓑ the store owner with the new skateboards
- Ⓒ his mother, who had heard about it
- Ⓓ Lee's friends who were skateboarding

**5.** What did Lee do to pay for his skateboard?
- Ⓐ borrowed money from his friends
- Ⓑ asked his mother for money to pay for it
- 🅒 traded used sports equipment for it
- Ⓓ worked hard after school to make money

GO ON



Benchmark 5



**Comprehension (continued)**

**6.** Lee brings all of the following to the Sixth Street store EXCEPT
- Ⓐ his mother's skies.
- 🅑 his aunt's football.
- Ⓒ things his brother had left behind.
- Ⓓ his old baseball equipment.

**7.** From this story, you can tell that
- Ⓐ Lee's mom worries about him skateboarding.
- Ⓑ Tamika knows a lot about skateboarding.
- Ⓒ Lee will not do well at skateboarding.
- 🅓 Tyree is a helpful and caring friend.

**8.** What did Tyree say would make the skateboard fast?
- Ⓐ greasing the wheels
- 🅑 its rubber wheels
- Ⓒ the rounded ends
- Ⓓ new metal wheels

**9.** How did Tyree help Lee out at the end?
- 🅐 Tyree gave Lee three dollars.
- Ⓑ Tyree showed Lee new moves.
- Ⓒ Tyree helped Lee fix a wheel.
- Ⓓ Tyree went to the park with Lee.

**10.** How can you tell that skateboarding is popular where Lee lives?
- Ⓐ Lee's friends spend time practicing their moves.
- Ⓑ Skateboards are sold at sporting goods stores.
- 🅒 The city built a park just for skateboarders.
- Ⓓ People can trade items for skateboards.

Benchmark 5



**Comprehension (continued)**

**1.** This selection is mostly about
- Ⓐ how Einstein changed physics.
- Ⓑ what school was like in Germany.
- 🅒 Einstein's struggles in school.
- Ⓓ becoming a famous scientist.

**2.** What did Einstein develop that changed the world's thinking?
- 🅐 theories about space and time
- Ⓑ ideas on how to get to the moon
- Ⓒ ways to make engines more efficient
- Ⓓ new approaches to art and science

**3.** Today, a student might be called an "Einstein" if he or she
- Ⓐ does very poorly in school.
- Ⓑ does not turn in homework.
- 🅒 is extremely intelligent.
- Ⓓ gives teachers trouble.

**4.** Einstein's teachers believed he was
- 🅐 not very smart.
- Ⓑ a brilliant student.
- Ⓒ a hard worker.
- Ⓓ always in trouble.

**5.** All of these were problems for Einstein in school EXCEPT
- Ⓐ he did not like to give quick answers.
- Ⓑ his teachers did not understand him.
- Ⓒ he only did work when he was interested in it.
- 🅓 he was not very smart, so he did poorly.

Benchmark 5



**Comprehension (continued)**

**6.** At age fifteen, all of these were problems for Einstein EXCEPT
- Ⓐ other students thought he was weird.
- Ⓑ his father's business was failing.
- Ⓒ his teachers thought little of him.
- 🅓 having to travel to the United States.

**7.** When his family moved to Italy, Einstein
- 🅐 dropped out of high school.
- Ⓑ stayed in Germany and finished high school.
- Ⓒ switched to a school in Italy.
- Ⓓ graduated from an Italian college.

**8.** What might have helped Einstein do better in school?
- Ⓐ having teachers who were stricter
- 🅑 having schoolwork that interested him
- Ⓒ having someone help him with his homework
- Ⓓ having more subjects to study

**9.** After Einstein became famous, he was amused that
- Ⓐ he was not smart, but he had done well in school.
- 🅑 his teachers always thought he could not learn.
- Ⓒ all the other students had thought he was weird.
- Ⓓ he had never remembered to do his homework.

**10.** One thing this selection shows you is that
- Ⓐ moving to another country helps solve problems.
- 🅑 students who do poorly can be successful later.
- Ⓒ teachers like students who give wrong answers.
- Ⓓ scientists have problems with schoolwork.

Benchmark 5

# Benchmark 5 Answer Sheets



## Vocabulary

**Read each item. Fill in the bubble for the answer you think is correct.**

1. Predict means
   - Ⓐ make things from long ago.
   - Ⓑ solve a problem.
   - Ⓒ write about people.
   - ● tell about the future.
2. Admire is the base word in admiration. Admiration means
   - ● respect.
   - Ⓑ fear.
   - Ⓒ explanation.
   - Ⓓ improvement.
3. Spectator means
   - Ⓐ a type of clock.
   - ● someone who watches.
   - Ⓒ large piles of sand.
   - Ⓓ strong winds.
4. What word means about the same as phase?
   - Ⓐ speech
   - Ⓑ trip
   - Ⓒ completion
   - ● stage
5. What word means about the same as delay?
   - Ⓐ play
   - ● wait
   - Ⓒ start
   - Ⓓ turn

GO ON



Benchmark 5



## Comprehension (continued)

6. What word means the opposite of clumsy?
   - Ⓐ awkward
   - ● graceful
   - Ⓑ tall
   - Ⓓ hungry
7. Which word BEST completes both sentences?

   **This ___ shows the cost of each car.**

   **Our ___ has wooden legs.**
   - ● table
   - Ⓒ tag
   - Ⓑ counter
   - Ⓓ desk
8. Which word BEST completes both sentences?

   **The ___ had a good game.**

   **Pour the orange juice from the ___.**
   - Ⓐ player
   - Ⓒ bottle
   - ● pitcher
   - Ⓓ team
9. The judge said she was innocent, so she was free to go. Innocent means.
   - Ⓐ young.
   - Ⓒ neglected.
   - Ⓑ understanding.
   - ● blameless.
10. The cows graze on the tasty grass in the field. Graze means
    - ● feed.
    - Ⓒ run.
    - Ⓑ sleep.
    - Ⓓ lie.

STOP



Benchmark 5



## Grammar, Usage, and Mechanics

**Read each question. Fill in the bubble beside the answer in each group that is correct. If none of the answers is correct, choose the last answer, "none of the above."**

1. Which sentence is written correctly?
   - Ⓐ His ancestors fought at gettysburg during the Civil War.
   - Ⓑ His Ancestors fought at Gettysburg during the civil war.
   - ● His ancestors fought at Gettysburg during the Civil War.
   - Ⓓ none of the above
2. Which sentence is written incorrectly?
   - ● Do not touch that red switch it's dangerous!
   - Ⓑ A friend touched the switch; he burned his finger.
   - Ⓒ There is one rule to follow: Leave the red switch alone!
   - Ⓓ none of the above
3. Which sentence is written incorrectly?
   - Ⓐ She did not see anything new.
   - Ⓑ I never miss any games.
   - ● Our team hardly never wins no games.
   - Ⓓ none of the above
4. Which sentence is written correctly?
   - Ⓐ "The director asked," Who will be at the concert?
   - Ⓑ The director asked, Who will be at the concert?
   - ● The director asked, "Who will be at the concert?"
   - Ⓓ none of the above
5. Which sentence is written correctly?
   - ● The drummer played the loudest of all the parade marchers.
   - Ⓑ The drummer played the most loudest of all the parade marchers.
   - Ⓒ The drummer played the most louder of all the parade marchers.
   - Ⓓ none of the above

GO ON



Benchmark 5



## Grammar, Usage, and Mechanics (continued)

6. Which sentence is written correctly?
   - Ⓐ I wants to be an astronaut like you.
   - ● The girl with the braids runs fast.
   - Ⓒ The smallest bird in the trees were chirping.
   - Ⓓ none of the above
7. Which sentence is written correctly?
   - Ⓐ She and him both wanted to walk to his store.
   - ● She and he both wanted to walk to his store.
   - Ⓒ Her and he both wanted walk to him store.
   - Ⓓ none of the above
8. Which sentence is written correctly?
   - Ⓐ The lion chased the zebra through the grass, but the zebra will get away.
   - Ⓑ The lion chases the zebra through the grass, but the zebra got away.
   - Ⓒ The lion will chase the zebra through the grass, but the zebra gets away.
   - ● none of the above
9. Which sentence is written correctly?
   - ● Paul helped the engineer make the machine work.
   - Ⓑ The machine with its many different cogs and wheels.
   - Ⓒ Paul's knowledge of machines and engines.
   - Ⓓ none of the above
10. What type of sentence is this?

    **As the Iron Age progressed, humans invented new tools.**
    - Ⓐ Simple
    - ● Complex
    - Ⓑ Compound
    - Ⓓ Not a sentence

STOP



Benchmark 5

# Benchmark 5 Answer Sheets

Benchmark 5

## Spelling

**Read each group of words. Only one of the words is spelled correctly. Fill in the bubble under the word that is spelled correctly.**

| | | | | |
|---|---|---|---|---|
| **1.** | frouth Ⓐ | forth Ⓑ | ferth Ⓒ | forht Ⓓ |
| **2.** | miosture Ⓐ | moystur Ⓑ | moisture Ⓒ | misture Ⓓ |
| **3.** | district Ⓐ | distrect Ⓑ | districk Ⓒ | distict Ⓓ |
| **4.** | opinar Ⓐ | openur Ⓑ | oponer Ⓒ | opener Ⓓ |
| **5.** | corts Ⓐ | courts Ⓑ | courst Ⓒ | curts Ⓓ |

GO ON



Benchmark 5

Benchmark 5

### Spelling (continued)

**In each sentence, look for the underlined word that is spelled incorrectly. Focus on just the underlined word. Fill in the bubble next to the sentence with the misspelled word. If all the underlined words are spelled correctly, choose "correct as is."**

**6.** Ⓐ The cowboy removed his horse's saddle.
Ⓑ Please glue these stars on that poster.
Ⓒ What is the diameter of a circle?
Ⓓ correct as is

**7.** Ⓐ The mayer gave a speech.
Ⓑ Our team was excited when we won.
Ⓒ Dad deposited a check in the bank.
Ⓓ correct as is

**8.** Ⓐ The ending of the movie was abrupt.
Ⓑ My dad is worried about the expanding town.
Ⓒ The river was too braod to wade across it.
Ⓓ correct as is

**9.** Ⓐ The ship dropped ancher in the harbor.
Ⓑ Does this make sense now?
Ⓒ He felt no hatred for the team.
Ⓓ correct as is

**10.** Ⓐ Joan writes in her journal once a week.
Ⓑ The children in the preschool are behaveing well.
Ⓒ Show respect for your parents!
Ⓓ correct as is

STOP **This is the end of the group-administered section of the Benchmark Assessment.**



Benchmark 5

Benchmark 5

Name ____________________ Date ________ Score ________

### Fluency MAZE Assessment

Kelly had been eagerly awaiting her favorite time of year. She checked the temperature every day **[mouth / until / socks]** at last, during the final week **[am / be / of]** March, the weather was warm enough. **[Key / The / Was]** family members put on warm clothes, **[gathered / possible / distract]** their supplies, and trekked into the **[woods / admit / later]**.

"Here's a tree that's big enough, Dad," Kelly **[author / inside / called]**.

Everyone hurried over to join her. **[Help / They / Name]** checked the tree for old scars, **[ivy / for / and]** then Dad drilled three holes in **[the / ill / was]** bark and tapped in spouts. Kelly **[now / and / get]** her mom hung buckets on the **[affect / spouts / enough]** and covered them. Now all they **[had / you / job]** to do was wait for the **[reverse / awesome / buckets]** to fill with sap.

When the **[buckets / whistle / someday]** were full, they collected them and **[carried / involve / weather]** them back to the house. Dad **[ant / try / lit]** the fire in the outdoor fireplace. **[Know / They / Rely]** did not make syrup in the **[problem / kitchen / emotion]** because boiling sap made too much steam. **[My / He / Dad]** rubbed a little oil around the **[rim / and / yet]** of the pot to help keep **[can / win / the]** sap from bubbling over. Then he **[jumper / poured / public]** some sap into the pot, and **[he / as / up]** the sap boiled down, he added **[wish / play / more]**.

Once it was done, they poured **[it / do / of]** into clean bottles. It was a **[cat / lot / but]** of work for such a little **[bit / all / end]** of syrup, but they thought **[top / hay / the]** effort was worth it, at least Kelly **[thought / struggle / fragile]** so.



Benchmark 5

**Comprehension (continued)**

1. This story is mostly about
   - Ⓐ a boy discovering his grandfather's secret.
   - Ⓑ a grandfather teaching his grandson to cook.
   - Ⓒ a boy who wants to win a chili cook-off.
   - Ⓓ a grandfather who has a secret recipe.
2. Why did Pappy refuse to write down the recipe?
   - Ⓐ He could not remember the ingredients.
   - Ⓑ He would not share a family secret.
   - Ⓒ He did not know how to write.
   - Ⓓ He had trouble writing with his stiff hands.
3. Pappy had the newspaper delivered
   - Ⓐ so no one would know he could not read.
   - Ⓑ because he wanted to keep up with the world news.
   - Ⓒ to compare it to the stories on television.
   - Ⓓ because it gave Bill something to read.
4. What did Bill offer to do for Pappy?
   - Ⓐ take the chili to the park for him
   - Ⓑ teach Pappy how to read and write
   - Ⓒ help Pappy improve the chili recipe
   - Ⓓ stir the chili so it would not burn
5. How did Pappy first respond to Bill's offer?
   - Ⓐ He did not want to try new things.
   - Ⓑ He did not have enough time to do it.
   - Ⓒ He was not at all interested in learning.
   - Ⓓ He thought he would not be good at it.

Benchmark 6



**Comprehension (continued)**

6. What did Bill ask Pappy to read?
   - Ⓐ a recipe from the chili cookbook
   - Ⓑ a story from that day's newspaper
   - Ⓒ a new book he had brought along
   - Ⓓ the sign for the Chili Cook-off
7. How did Pappy know what the words said?
   - Ⓐ Bill had read them to him before.
   - Ⓑ Pappy had seen them in another place.
   - Ⓒ Bill sounded out the words for Pappy.
   - Ⓓ Pappy sounded out each word.
8. From this story, you can tell that Bill
   - Ⓐ has never cooked chili before.
   - Ⓑ is very upset with his grandfather.
   - Ⓒ cares a lot about his grandfather.
   - Ⓓ will not win the Chili Cook-off.
9. Why do you think Pappy hid his secret from people?
   - Ⓐ It had just happened recently.
   - Ⓑ He was embarrassed about it.
   - Ⓒ He had always been very shy.
   - Ⓓ It was not important to him.
10. When Bill breathed the air in the kitchen, how might it have smelled?
    - Ⓐ very spicy
    - Ⓑ cool and lemony
    - Ⓒ sweet like candy
    - Ⓓ like spring flowers

Benchmark 6



**Comprehension (continued)**

1. This selection is mostly about
   - Ⓐ why Stonehenge was built in ancient times.
   - Ⓑ who built Stonehenge and how they did it.
   - Ⓒ why Stonehenge still remains a mystery.
   - Ⓓ how all the huge stones got to Stonehenge.
2. When do scientists estimate that the earliest parts were built?
   - Ⓐ 8000 B.C. to 2000 B.C.
   - Ⓑ 30,000 B.C. to 20,000 B.C.
   - Ⓒ 1000 A.D. to 1500 A.D.
   - Ⓓ 200 B.C. to 800 A.D.
3. How did the earlier parts differ from the later parts?
   - Ⓐ First stones were put in a circle, then mounds were added.
   - Ⓑ First the stones were put up, then wood was added.
   - Ⓒ First people lived there, then they buried people there.
   - Ⓓ First it was wood and earth, then the stones were added.
4. Where did the bluestones come from?
   - Ⓐ from the nearby mountains and lakes
   - Ⓑ from a hundred miles away in Wales
   - Ⓒ from glaciers shaping them long ago
   - Ⓓ from a quarry twenty-four miles away
5. When huge stones were put on a model of an ancient boat in 2001,
   - Ⓐ the boat floated low in the water.
   - Ⓑ the stones arrived a few at a time.
   - Ⓒ the boat sank after it was loaded.
   - Ⓓ the stones could not fit on deck.

Benchmark 6



**Comprehension (continued)**

6. To build Stonehenge, people did NOT need to know
   - Ⓐ where to find all the large stones.
   - Ⓑ how to transport such heavy stones.
   - Ⓒ how to lift such heavy loads.
   - Ⓓ how to lay bricks to build houses.
7. The reason some people believe Stonehenge was a burial ground is that
   - Ⓐ the stones have dates on them.
   - Ⓑ bodies are buried in the area.
   - Ⓒ they found many burial tools.
   - Ⓓ old records show it was.
8. What do some people believe Stonehenge was used for?
   - Ⓐ predicting movements of bodies in space
   - Ⓑ as a quarry for digging up huge stones
   - Ⓒ a port for transporting goods by boat
   - Ⓓ an ancient village of homes and stores
9. From this selection, you can tell that the builders of Stonehenge
   - Ⓐ used very primitive building methods.
   - Ⓑ did not make it very well, as it is now in ruins.
   - Ⓒ did something that was very difficult.
   - Ⓓ knew very little about how to work with stone.
10. A good title for this selection is
    - Ⓐ "Ancient Machines."
    - Ⓑ "Rock Climbing."
    - Ⓒ "The Mysteries of Stonehenge."
    - Ⓓ "A Visit to England."

STOP



Benchmark 6

# Benchmark 6 Answer Sheets

Benchmark 6

## Vocabulary

**Read each item. Fill in the bubble for the answer you think is correct.**

1. Disagree means
   - Ⓐ move over.
   - Ⓑ line up.
   - Ⓒ respect.
   - ● differ.

2. Produce is the base word in overproduction. Overproduction means
   - Ⓐ full of pain.
   - ● more than needed.
   - Ⓒ without money.
   - Ⓓ almost finished.

3. A telescope helps you
   - ● see things that are far away.
   - Ⓑ hear things that are said softly.
   - Ⓒ speak to people across the world.
   - Ⓓ write letters and notes.

4. What word means about the same as filthy?
   - Ⓐ happy
   - Ⓑ spotless
   - ● dirty
   - Ⓓ tired

5. What word means about the same as handy?
   - Ⓐ hopeless
   - Ⓑ clumsy
   - Ⓒ busy
   - ● useful

GO ON

Benchmark Assessment • Benchmark 6 Level 5 • 97

**Benchmark 6**

Benchmark 6

## Vocabulary (continued)

6. What word means the opposite of bitter?
   - Ⓐ earlier
   - Ⓑ salty
   - ● happy
   - Ⓓ harsh

7. Which word BEST completes both sentences?

   **The school ___ met yesterday.**

   **Please hand me the ___ I just cut.**
   - Ⓐ group
   - ● board
   - Ⓒ log
   - Ⓓ committee

8. Which word BEST completes both sentences?

   **The runner began to ___.**

   **That ___ is still a little low.**
   - Ⓐ sweat
   - Ⓑ car
   - ● tire
   - Ⓓ turn

9. The ice storm made the trip home perilous. Perilous means
   - Ⓐ blinding.
   - ● dangerous.
   - Ⓒ long.
   - Ⓓ slippery.

10. Since his directions were vague, we got lost. Vague means
    - Ⓐ spoken.
    - Ⓑ good.
    - Ⓒ long.
    - ● unclear.

STOP

98 • Level 5 Benchmark Assessment • Benchmark 6

**Benchmark 6**

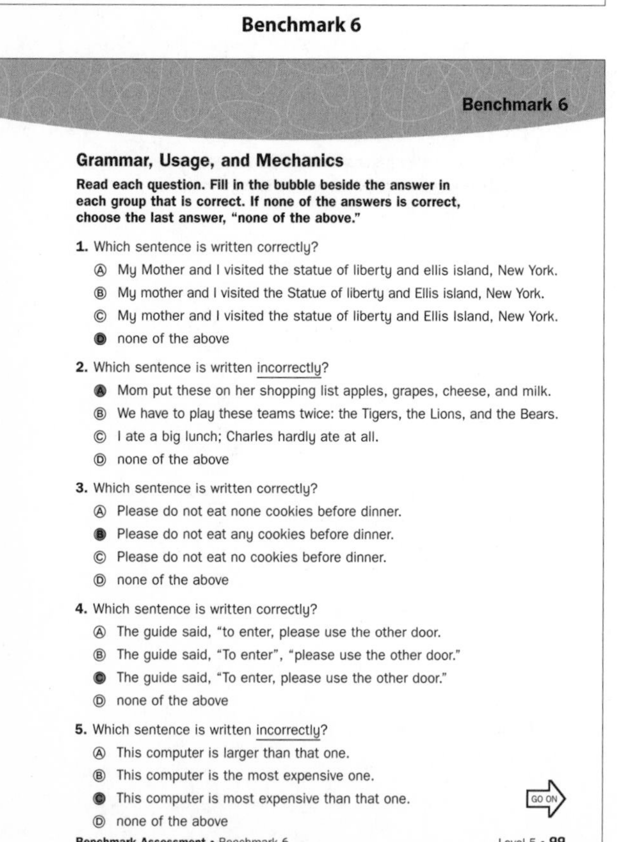

Benchmark 6

## Grammar, Usage, and Mechanics

**Read each question. Fill in the bubble beside the answer in each group that is correct. If none of the answers is correct, choose the last answer, "none of the above."**

1. Which sentence is written correctly?
   - Ⓐ My Mother and I visited the statue of liberty and ellis island, New York.
   - Ⓑ My mother and I visited the Statue of liberty and Ellis island, New York.
   - Ⓒ My mother and I visited the statue of liberty and Ellis Island, New York.
   - ● none of the above

2. Which sentence is written incorrectly?
   - ● Mom put these on her shopping list apples, grapes, cheese, and milk.
   - Ⓑ We have to play these teams twice: the Tigers, the Lions, and the Bears.
   - Ⓒ I ate a big lunch; Charles hardly ate at all.
   - Ⓓ none of the above

3. Which sentence is written correctly?
   - Ⓐ Please do not eat none cookies before dinner.
   - ● Please do not eat any cookies before dinner.
   - Ⓒ Please do not eat no cookies before dinner.
   - Ⓓ none of the above

4. Which sentence is written correctly?
   - Ⓐ The guide said, "to enter, please use the other door.
   - Ⓑ The guide said, "To enter", "please use the other door."
   - ● The guide said, "To enter, please use the other door."
   - Ⓓ none of the above

5. Which sentence is written incorrectly?
   - Ⓐ This computer is larger than that one.
   - Ⓑ This computer is the most expensive one.
   - ● This computer is most expensive than that one.
   - Ⓓ none of the above

GO ON

Benchmark Assessment • Benchmark 6 Level 5 • 99

**Benchmark 6**

Benchmark 6

## Grammar, Usage, and Mechanics (continued)

6. Which sentence is written correctly?
   - ● In ancient China, only emperors were allowed to wear yellow.
   - Ⓑ Only emperors in ancient China was allowed to wear yellow.
   - Ⓒ In ancient China, only emperors was allowed to wear yellow.
   - Ⓓ none of the above

7. Which sentence is written correctly?
   - Ⓐ You can help yourself to them salad and bread.
   - ● You can help yourself to their salad and bread.
   - Ⓒ You can help you to they salad and bread.
   - Ⓓ none of the above

8. Which sentence is written correctly?
   - Ⓐ Josh will handle the film, and Jim carried the camera.
   - Ⓑ Josh handled the film, and Jim carries the camera.
   - ● Josh will handle the film, and Jim will carry the camera.
   - Ⓓ none of the above

9. Which sentence is written correctly?
   - Ⓐ Five people with their bags beside them.
   - Ⓑ The train to Paris and also to London.
   - Ⓒ The people's large suitcases and many other packages.
   - ● none of the above

10. What type of sentence is this?

    **Penny has played soccer for many years, and we think she should be captain.**
    - Ⓐ Simple
    - ● Compound
    - Ⓒ Complex
    - Ⓓ Not a sentence

STOP

100 • Level 5 Benchmark Assessment • Benchmark 6

**Benchmark 6**

## Spelling

**Read each group of words. Only one of the words is spelled correctly. Fill in the bubble under the word that is spelled correctly.**

| | | | | |
|---|---|---|---|---|
| 1. | activities ● | aktivities Ⓑ | asctiveties Ⓒ | activiteis Ⓓ |
| 2. | eccsuse Ⓐ | ecuse Ⓑ | excuse ● | axcuse Ⓓ |
| 3. | campayn Ⓐ | campaign ● | cempaign Ⓒ | campain Ⓓ |
| 4. | ativate Ⓐ | activat Ⓑ | actavate Ⓒ | activate ● |
| 5. | plainly ● | playnley Ⓑ | planly Ⓒ | palinly Ⓓ |

Benchmark 6



## Spelling (continued)

**In each sentence, look for the underlined word that is spelled incorrectly. Focus on just the underlined word. Fill in the bubble next to the sentence with the misspelled word. If all the underlined words are spelled correctly, choose "correct as is."**

6. Ⓐ The fabric for the curtain is <u>sheer</u>.
   Ⓑ Instructions are <u>attached</u> to the new television.
   Ⓒ Waiting for Trey <u>delayed</u> us.
   ● correct as is
7. Ⓐ José gave a <u>groan</u> when they scored.
   ● Dyan let me borrow her new <u>sweatter</u>.
   Ⓒ The baseball flew through the window <u>pane</u>.
   Ⓓ correct as is
8. Ⓐ The <u>gravel</u> road was bumpy.
   Ⓑ Our class wants to <u>publish</u> a newsletter.
   ● A pencil and notebook are <u>esential</u> for taking notes.
   Ⓓ correct as is
9. Ⓐ Pete <u>drew</u> cars and monsters on his paper.
   Ⓑ Susan <u>mowed</u> the grass for the neighbors.
   ● Smelling flowers makes Brian <u>sneaze</u>.
   Ⓓ correct as is
10. ● Tomato juice helps with a skunk's <u>oder</u>.
   Ⓑ Hiking this trail can be <u>difficult</u>.
   Ⓒ Dad saw if the locks were <u>secure</u>.
   Ⓓ correct as is

**This is the end of the group-administered section of the Benchmark Assessment.**



Benchmark 6



**Name** ______________________ **Date** ________ **Score** ________

## Fluency MAZE Assessment

Things kept disappearing. Mary thought there must be a **[purse / thief / add]** in the neighborhood. First it was Aunt Becky's pie **[left / feel / rush]** on the porch ledge to cool. **[The / Gap / Use]** pan had been licked clean and **[stay / hand / then]** dropped on the porch. Next, it **[lie / was / rub]** a basket of apples. The thief **[was / toy / ram]** in a hurry because pieces of **[ready / meant / apple]** were still on the ground. Mary **[diplomat / followed / presence]** the trail to the grass and **[incline / perfect / studied]** the ground like she'd seen detectives **[at / do / me]** on television, but found no more **[backfire / evidence / decision]**. The thief must have gone through **[the / fur / pal]** grass toward the barnyard or pasture. **[Fun / Lip / She]** searched the dusty ground for footprints, **[its / but / zoo]** only found chicken tracks and goat **[hoof / knew / lean]** prints, and those were always there.

**[There / Ready / Chest]** had to be a way to **[last / wild / find]** out who was stealing things. The **[only / rely / were]** thing the two crimes had in **[common / nation / across]** was that they were related to food, so Mary **[experts / balance / decided]** to trap the thief with food.

**[Guess / Blame / Early]** the next morning, Mary put some **[truck / fruit / blame]** on a plate and set it on **[the / than / because]** ledge, then crouched down inside **[to / up / we]** wait. Suddenly, the plate crashed to **[bay / one / the]** porch. Mary rushed to the window **[as / in / by]** time to see one of the **[meant / about / goats]** trotting off the porch. She had **[solved / couple / choice]** the mystery, and all that was **[miss / rush / left]** was to convince Aunt Becky to **[till / stop / adds]** putting food on the windowsill.



Benchmark 6

# Benchmark 7 Answer Sheets

**Benchmark 7**

**Comprehension (continued)**

**1.** This story is mostly about
🅐 a boy trying to learn new customs.
Ⓑ how to wrap a birthday gift properly.
Ⓒ why people are sometimes impatient.
Ⓓ a boy who learns a new language.

**2.** Erik and Semir go shopping for
Ⓐ basketball uniforms.
Ⓑ wrapping paper.
🅒 Jenna's present.
Ⓓ a birthday cake.

**3.** Why did Erik not go to the party with Semir?
Ⓐ He went there early to help Jenna decorate.
Ⓑ His parents did not allow him to go to parties.
Ⓒ He was going there with his other friends.
🅓 He went to his brother's basketball game first.

**4.** How did Semir wrap the gift to surprise Jenna?
Ⓐ He used fancy paper and bows.
🅑 He left it in the store bag.
Ⓒ He decorated a special box.
Ⓓ He got a birthday gift bag.

**5.** Why was Jenna surprised by Semir's card?
Ⓐ He had picked one that made her laugh.
Ⓑ It was written in another language.
Ⓒ His card was bigger than all the others.
🅓 It was not signed or in its envelope.

**108** • Level 5 **Benchmark Assessment** • Benchmark 7

**Benchmark 7**

**Benchmark 7**

**Comprehension (continued)**

**6.** Erik tried to make Semir feel better in all these ways EXCEPT
Ⓐ he told everyone the card could be recycled.
Ⓑ he apologized for not explaining about cards.
🅒 he invited him to play basketball with him.
Ⓓ he said wrapping paper was only thrown away.

**7.** From this story, you can tell that Erik
🅐 was a kind and caring person.
Ⓑ preferred basketball to parties.
Ⓒ did not know Jenna very well.
Ⓓ did not have many friends.

**8.** At the end, Jenna realized that it was
Ⓐ time for everyone to leave.
Ⓑ hard to make friends.
Ⓒ fun to get so many gifts.
🅓 difficult to learn new customs.

**9.** How did Semir feel when Jenna opened her other gifts and cards?
Ⓐ jealous that Jenna got them
🅑 embarrassed about his mistake
Ⓒ happy that she got nice gifts
Ⓓ curious to see what she got

**10.** What will Semir, Jenna, and Erik probably talk about during the walk home?
Ⓐ basketball
Ⓑ school subjects
🅒 other customs
Ⓓ Jenna's gifts

**Benchmark Assessment** • Benchmark 7 Level 5 • **109**

**Benchmark 7**

**Benchmark 7**

**Comprehension (continued)**

**1.** This selection is mostly about
Ⓐ the many different engines women invented.
🅑 the difficulties women had getting patents.
Ⓒ how to do the research needed for a patent.
Ⓓ why few women had money of their own.

**2.** What happened to many women's inventions long ago?
Ⓐ Their patents were never recorded.
Ⓑ Most of them did not work well.
Ⓒ Women never invented anything.
🅓 Men often took credit for them.

**3.** Which of these is NOT needed for a patent?
Ⓐ proof that you are the first to think of the idea
Ⓑ drawings to show how the invention works
Ⓒ proof that the idea works and will be useful
🅓 a bill showing how much it will cost to make

**4.** Why did most women invent household items?
Ⓐ They were not allowed to do other things.
🅑 Most women worked in the home.
Ⓒ Men never invented anything for the home.
Ⓓ There was no need for other types of inventions.

**5.** Attitudes toward women affected how many patents they got by
🅐 making them feel it was unacceptable to invent things.
Ⓑ encouraging them to learn about engines and science.
Ⓒ teaching them to take credit for the things they made.
Ⓓ giving them many opportunities to try new things.

**112** • Level 5 **Benchmark Assessment** • Benchmark 7

**Benchmark 7**

**Benchmark 7**

**Comprehension (continued)**

**6.** Women did not get patents for all these reasons EXCEPT
Ⓐ it was too expensive.
🅑 only men could get patents.
Ⓒ they mainly stayed home.
Ⓓ they could not do research.

**7.** What did Sarah Mather design?
🅐 a submarine telescope and lamp
Ⓑ a machine to wash dishes
Ⓒ a steering device for a boat
Ⓓ a sonar detector for the ocean

**8.** From this selection, you can tell that women who got patents
Ⓐ did not do anything with their patents.
Ⓑ had a hard time selling their inventions.
Ⓒ could not have a home and family, too.
🅓 had to overcome many obstacles.

**9.** Women were likely to get patents for all these things EXCEPT
Ⓐ better clothing and stoves.
Ⓑ new sewing thread and irons.
Ⓒ a new weaving process.
🅓 car and truck engines.

**10.** Sarah Mather's invention was unique because
Ⓐ women could only design things for their houses.
Ⓑ no one knows much about her or her life.
🅒 most women then did not know about machines.
Ⓓ she had no opportunity to research patents.

**Benchmark Assessment** • Benchmark 7 Level 5 • **113**

**Benchmark 7**

# Benchmark 7 Answer Sheets



## Vocabulary

**Read each item. Fill in the bubble for the answer you think is correct.**

1. Descendant means
   - Ⓐ a group that protects old buildings.
   - Ⓑ a scientist who studies the deep ocean.
   - ● a person related to a person in the past.
   - Ⓓ a meeting that took place long ago.
2. Obey is the base word in disobey. Disobey means
   - Ⓐ leave a place.
   - ● not follow a rule.
   - Ⓒ meet with.
   - Ⓓ do something twice.
3. A biography is
   - ● a life story.
   - Ⓑ the science of life.
   - Ⓒ a math formula.
   - Ⓓ a machine.
4. What word means about the same as condensed?
   - Ⓐ extended
   - Ⓑ perplexed
   - Ⓒ attached
   - ● shortened
5. What word means about the same as slack?
   - Ⓐ shiny
   - Ⓑ complete
   - ● loose
   - Ⓓ tight

GO ON



Benchmark 7



### Vocabulary (continued)

6. What word means the opposite of definitely?
   - ● possibly
   - Ⓑ surely
   - Ⓒ thoroughly
   - Ⓓ lately
7. Which word BEST completes both sentences?
   **I can finish it in a ____.**
   **The lightning ____ frightened us.**
   - Ⓐ hurry
   - Ⓑ bolt
   - ● flash
   - Ⓓ rod
8. Which word BEST completes both sentences?
   **Allen ____ a hole into the wood.**
   **We were ____ waiting for the train.**
   - Ⓐ drilled
   - Ⓑ cold
   - ● bored
   - Ⓓ busy
9. The modest girl did not want to accept the award. Modest means
   - ● shy.
   - Ⓑ little.
   - Ⓒ sleepy.
   - Ⓓ pretty.
10. Many children are transported to school by a bus. Transported means
    - ● carried.
    - Ⓑ accepted.
    - Ⓒ attached.
    - Ⓓ helped.

STOP



Benchmark 7

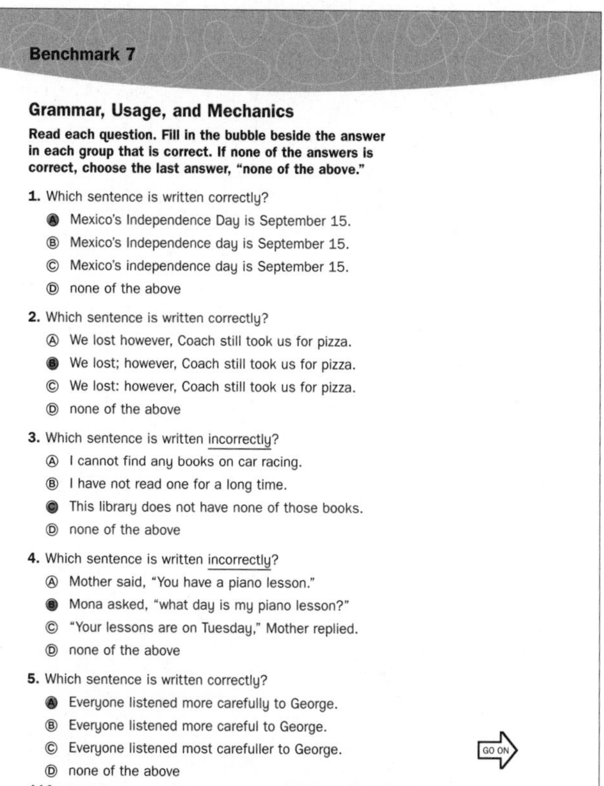



## Grammar, Usage, and Mechanics

**Read each question. Fill in the bubble beside the answer in each group that is correct. If none of the answers is correct, choose the last answer, "none of the above."**

1. Which sentence is written correctly?
   - ● Mexico's Independence Day is September 15.
   - Ⓑ Mexico's Independence day is September 15.
   - Ⓒ Mexico's independence day is September 15.
   - Ⓓ none of the above
2. Which sentence is written correctly?
   - Ⓐ We lost however, Coach still took us for pizza.
   - ● We lost; however, Coach still took us for pizza.
   - Ⓒ We lost: however, Coach still took us for pizza.
   - Ⓓ none of the above
3. Which sentence is written incorrectly?
   - Ⓐ I cannot find any books on car racing.
   - Ⓑ I have not read one for a long time.
   - ● This library does not have none of those books.
   - Ⓓ none of the above
4. Which sentence is written incorrectly?
   - Ⓐ Mother said, "You have a piano lesson."
   - ● Mona asked, "what day is my piano lesson?"
   - Ⓒ "Your lessons are on Tuesday," Mother replied.
   - Ⓓ none of the above
5. Which sentence is written correctly?
   - ● Everyone listened more carefully to George.
   - Ⓑ Everyone listened more careful to George.
   - Ⓒ Everyone listened most carefuller to George.
   - Ⓓ none of the above

GO ON



Benchmark 7



### Grammar, Usage, and Mechanics (continued)

6. Which sentence is written correctly?
   - Ⓐ Herb were blowing a whistle to call everyone together.
   - Ⓑ Herb, to call everyone together, were blowing a whistle.
   - ● To call everyone together, Herb was blowing a whistle.
   - Ⓓ none of the above
7. Which sentence is written correctly?
   - Ⓐ I and Devon went shopping at the mall.
   - Ⓑ Devon and me went shopping at the mall.
   - Ⓒ Me and Devon went shopping at the mall.
   - ● none of the above
8. Which sentence is written correctly?
   - Ⓐ Mom uses the machine outside when the lines were too long in the bank.
   - Ⓑ Lines inside the bank will be too long, so Mom used the machine outside.
   - ● Lines inside the bank were too long, so Mom used the machine outside.
   - Ⓓ none of the above
9. Which sentence is written correctly?
   - Ⓐ Too much water in the air and warm weather in summer.
   - ● Before the storm began, black clouds formed overhead.
   - Ⓒ Huge black clouds heavy with plenty of raindrops.
   - Ⓓ none of the above
10. What type of sentence is this?
    **That glass and this pitcher need to be washed and dried.**
    - ● Simple
    - Ⓑ Compound
    - Ⓒ Complex
    - Ⓓ Not a sentence

STOP



Benchmark 7

# Benchmark 7 Answer Sheets



## Spelling

**Read each group of words. Only one of the words is spelled correctly. Fill in the bubble under the word that is spelled correctly.**

| | | | | |
|---|---|---|---|---|
| **1.** | socs | socks | sokcs | soks |
| | Ⓐ | ● | Ⓒ | Ⓓ |
| **2.** | curtian | cutrain | curtain | crutain |
| | Ⓐ | Ⓑ | ● | Ⓓ |
| **3.** | drizel | drizzel | drizzul | drizzle |
| | Ⓐ | Ⓑ | Ⓒ | ● |
| **4.** | bowndry | boundary | boondary | boyndary |
| | Ⓐ | ● | Ⓒ | Ⓓ |
| **5.** | spacecraft | spacecarft | spacecraf | spasecraft |
| | ● | Ⓑ | Ⓒ | Ⓓ |

GO ON



Benchmark 7



## Spelling (continued)

**In each sentence, look for the underlined word that is spelled incorrectly. Focus on just the underlined word. Fill in the bubble next to the sentence with the misspelled word. If all the underlined words are spelled correctly, choose "correct as is."**

**6.** Ⓐ It took fifteen gallons of gasoline to fill the tank.
Ⓑ The distance to town is about ten miles.
● Some medicines may cause diziness.
Ⓓ correct as is

**7.** Ⓐ Paul is accustomed to waiting for Drew.
Ⓑ Do you like this pattern for the chair covers?
Ⓒ Vera claims she should go first.
● correct as is

**8.** Ⓐ Deb bought material for a new dress.
● Would you like to go for a sliegh ride?
Ⓒ Mia debates on our school team.
Ⓓ correct as is

**9.** Ⓐ The new worker had prior experience.
Ⓑ The park is public property.
● Did you relize it is time to go?
Ⓓ correct as is

**10.** Ⓐ Can I depend on you to finish the job?
Ⓑ Latoya picked out the perfume.
Ⓒ The beating of the heart is automatic.
● correct as is

**This is the end of the group-administered section of the Benchmark Assessment.**



Benchmark 7

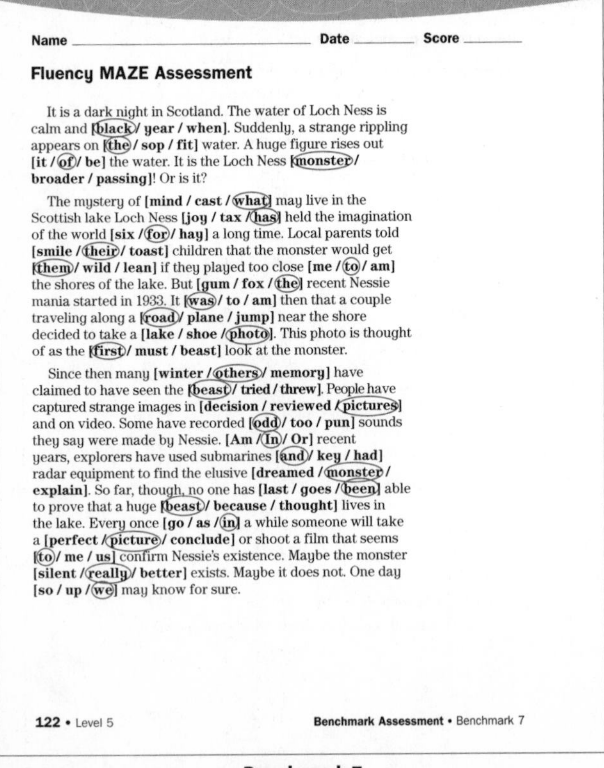

Benchmark 7

Name ______ Date ______ Score ______

**Fluency MAZE Assessment**

It is a dark night in Scotland. The water of Loch Ness is calm and **[black / year / when]**. Suddenly, a strange rippling appears on **[the / sop / fit]** water. A huge figure rises out **[it / of / be]** the water. It is the Loch Ness **[monster / broader / passing]**! Or is it?

The mystery of **[mind / cast / what]** may live in the Scottish lake Loch Ness **[joy / tax / has]** held the imagination of the world **[six / for / hay]** a long time. Local parents told **[smile / their / toast]** children that the monster would get **[them / wild / lean]** if they played too close **[me / to / am]** the shores of the lake. But **[gum / fox / the]** recent Nessie mania started in 1933. It **[was / to / am]** then that a couple traveling along a **[road / plane / jump]** near the shore decided to take a **[lake / shoe / photo]**. This photo is thought of as the **[first / must / beast]** look at the monster.

Since then many **[winter / others / memory]** have claimed to have seen the **[beast / tried / threw]**. People have captured strange images in **[decision / reviewed / pictures]** and on video. Some have recorded **[odd / too / pun]** sounds they say were made by Nessie. **[Am / In / Or]** recent years, explorers have used submarines **[and / key / had]** radar equipment to find the elusive **[dreamed / monster / explain]**. So far, though, no one has **[last / goes / been]** able to prove that a huge **[beast / because / thought]** lives in the lake. Every once **[go / as / in]** a while someone will take a **[perfect / picture / conclude]** or shoot a film that seems **[to / me / us]** confirm Nessie's existence. Maybe the monster **[silent / really / better]** exists. Maybe it does not. One day **[so / up / we]** may know for sure.

122 • Level 5 Benchmark Assessment • Benchmark 7

Benchmark 7

Benchmark 1

# Four Point Rubrics for Expository Writing

| Genre | 1 Point | 2 Points | 3 Points | 4 Points |
|---|---|---|---|---|
| **Expository** | Composition has no introduction or clear topic. It offers a group of loosely related facts or a series of poorly written steps. No conclusion is included. | Composition is clearly organized around main points with supportive facts or assertions. Composition has no clear introduction, but its topic is identifiable. However, it includes many facts unrelated to the topic, or it describes things in a disorganized way. No conclusion is included. | Main points and supportive details can be identified, but they are not clearly marked. Composition has an introduction and offers facts about the topic. Some facts may be irrelevant, or some ideas may be vague or out of order. The report is fairly well organized but doesn't have a strong conclusion. | Traces and constructs a line of argument, identifying part-to-whole relations. Main points are supported with logical and appropriate evidence. Composition begins with an introduction and offers relevant facts about the topic or describes the topic appropriately. The report is organized using cause/effect, comparison/contrast, or another pattern. It ends with a strong conclusion |
| **Writing Traits** | | | | |
| **Focus** | Topic is unclear or wanders and must be inferred. Extraneous material may be present. | Topic/position/direction is unclear and must be inferred. | Topic/position is stated and direction/ purpose is previewed and maintained. Mainly stays on topic. | Topic/position is clearly stated, previewed, and maintained throughout the paper. Topics and details are tied together with a central theme or purpose that is maintained /threaded throughout the paper. |
| **Ideas/Content** | Superficial and/or minimal content is included. | Main ideas are understandable, although they may be overly broad or simplistic, and the results may not be effective. Supporting detail is limited, insubstantial, overly general or off topic. | The writing is clear and focused. The reader can easily understand the main ideas. Support is present, although it may be limited or rather general. | Writing is exceptionally clear, focused, and interesting. Main ideas stand out and are developed by strong support and rich details. |
| **Elaboration (supporting details and examples that develop the main idea)** | States ideas or points with minimal detail to support them. | Includes sketchy, redundant, or general details; some may be irrelevant. Support for key ideas is very uneven. | Includes mix of general statements and specific details/examples. Support is mostly relevant but may be uneven and lack depth in places. | Includes specific details and supporting examples for each key point/idea. May use compare/contrast to support. |
| **Writing Conventions** | | | | |
| **Conventions Overall** | Numerous errors in usage, grammar, spelling, capitalization, and punctuation repeatedly distract the reader and make the text difficult to read. The reader finds it difficult to focus on the message. | The writing demonstrates limited control of standard writing conventions (punctuation, spelling, capitalization, grammar, and usage). Errors sometimes impede readability. | The writing demonstrates control of standard writing conventions (punctuation, spelling, capitalization, grammar, and usage). Minor errors, while perhaps noticeable, do not impede readability. | The writing demonstrates exceptionally strong control of standard writing conventions (punctuation, spelling, capitalization, grammar, and usage) and uses them effectively to enhance communication. Errors are so few and so minor that the reader can easily skim over them. |

# Benchmark Assessment Record

| Student Name | Comprehension (40 points) | Vocabulary (30 points) | Grammar, Usage, and Mechanics (20 points) | Spelling (10 points) | Total Score | Cutoff Reached? (20 points) | Fluency (WPM or MAZE total) | Cutoff Reached? (85 or 12) | Writing Prompt Cutoff Reached? |
|---|---|---|---|---|---|---|---|---|---|
| | | | | | | | | | |
| | | | | | | | | | |
| | | | | | | | | | |
| | | | | | | | | | |
| | | | | | | | | | |
| | | | | | | | | | |
| | | | | | | | | | |
| | | | | | | | | | |
| | | | | | | | | | |
| | | | | | | | | | |
| | | | | | | | | | |
| | | | | | | | | | |
| | | | | | | | | | |
| | | | | | | | | | |
| | | | | | | | | | |
| | | | | | | | | | |
| | | | | | | | | | |
| | | | | | | | | | |
| | | | | | | | | | |
| | | | | | | | | | |
| | | | | | | | | | |

# Benchmark Assessment Record

| Student Name | Comprehension (40 points) | Vocabulary (30 points) | Grammar, Usage, and Mechanics (20 points) | Spelling (10 points) | Total Score | Cutoff Reached? (30 points) | Fluency (WPM or MAZE total) | Cutoff Reached? (98 or 13) |
|---|---|---|---|---|---|---|---|---|
| | | | | | | | | |
| | | | | | | | | |
| | | | | | | | | |
| | | | | | | | | |
| | | | | | | | | |
| | | | | | | | | |
| | | | | | | | | |
| | | | | | | | | |
| | | | | | | | | |
| | | | | | | | | |
| | | | | | | | | |
| | | | | | | | | |
| | | | | | | | | |
| | | | | | | | | |
| | | | | | | | | |
| | | | | | | | | |
| | | | | | | | | |
| | | | | | | | | |
| | | | | | | | | |
| | | | | | | | | |
| | | | | | | | | |

# Benchmark Assessment Record

| Student Name | Comprehension (40 points) | Vocabulary (30 points) | Grammar, Usage, and Mechanics (20 points) | Spelling (10 points) | Total Score | Cutoff Reached? (42 points) | Fluency (WPM or MAZE total) | Cutoff Reached? (112 or 14) |
|---|---|---|---|---|---|---|---|---|
| | | | | | | | | |
| | | | | | | | | |
| | | | | | | | | |
| | | | | | | | | |
| | | | | | | | | |
| | | | | | | | | |
| | | | | | | | | |
| | | | | | | | | |
| | | | | | | | | |
| | | | | | | | | |
| | | | | | | | | |
| | | | | | | | | |
| | | | | | | | | |
| | | | | | | | | |
| | | | | | | | | |
| | | | | | | | | |
| | | | | | | | | |
| | | | | | | | | |
| | | | | | | | | |
| | | | | | | | | |
| | | | | | | | | |

# Benchmark Assessment Record

| Student Name | Comprehension (40 points) | Vocabulary (30 points) | Grammar, Usage, and Mechanics (20 points) | Spelling (10 points) | Total Score | Cutoff Reached? (54 points) | Fluency (WPM or MAZE total) | Cutoff Reached? (126 or 15) | Writing Prompt Cutoff Reached? |
|---|---|---|---|---|---|---|---|---|---|
| | | | | | | | | | |
| | | | | | | | | | |
| | | | | | | | | | |
| | | | | | | | | | |
| | | | | | | | | | |
| | | | | | | | | | |
| | | | | | | | | | |
| | | | | | | | | | |
| | | | | | | | | | |
| | | | | | | | | | |
| | | | | | | | | | |
| | | | | | | | | | |
| | | | | | | | | | |
| | | | | | | | | | |
| | | | | | | | | | |
| | | | | | | | | | |
| | | | | | | | | | |
| | | | | | | | | | |
| | | | | | | | | | |
| | | | | | | | | | |
| | | | | | | | | | |

# Benchmark Assessment Record

| Student Name | Comprehension (40 points) | Vocabulary (30 points) | Grammar, Usage, and Mechanics (20 points) | Spelling (10 points) | Total Score | Cutoff Reached? (66 points) | Fluency (WPM or MAZE total) | Cutoff Reached? (140 or 16) |
|---|---|---|---|---|---|---|---|---|
| | | | | | | | | |
| | | | | | | | | |
| | | | | | | | | |
| | | | | | | | | |
| | | | | | | | | |
| | | | | | | | | |
| | | | | | | | | |
| | | | | | | | | |
| | | | | | | | | |
| | | | | | | | | |
| | | | | | | | | |
| | | | | | | | | |
| | | | | | | | | |
| | | | | | | | | |
| | | | | | | | | |
| | | | | | | | | |
| | | | | | | | | |
| | | | | | | | | |
| | | | | | | | | |
| | | | | | | | | |
| | | | | | | | | |

# Benchmark Assessment Record

| Student Name | Comprehension (40 points) | Vocabulary (30 points) | Grammar, Usage, and Mechanics (20 points) | Spelling (10 points) | Total Score | Cutoff Reached? (78 points) | Fluency (WPM or MAZE total) | Cutoff Reached? (154 or 17) |
|---|---|---|---|---|---|---|---|---|
| | | | | | | | | |
| | | | | | | | | |
| | | | | | | | | |
| | | | | | | | | |
| | | | | | | | | |
| | | | | | | | | |
| | | | | | | | | |
| | | | | | | | | |
| | | | | | | | | |
| | | | | | | | | |
| | | | | | | | | |
| | | | | | | | | |
| | | | | | | | | |
| | | | | | | | | |
| | | | | | | | | |
| | | | | | | | | |
| | | | | | | | | |
| | | | | | | | | |
| | | | | | | | | |
| | | | | | | | | |

# Benchmark Assessment Record

| Student Name | Comprehension (40 points) | Vocabulary (30 points) | Grammar, Usage, and Mechanics (20 points) | Spelling (10 points) | Total Score | Cutoff Reached? (90 points) | Fluency (WPM or MAZE total) | Cutoff Reached? (168 or 18) | Writing Prompt Cutoff Reached? |
|---|---|---|---|---|---|---|---|---|---|
| | | | | | | | | | |
| | | | | | | | | | |
| | | | | | | | | | |
| | | | | | | | | | |
| | | | | | | | | | |
| | | | | | | | | | |
| | | | | | | | | | |
| | | | | | | | | | |
| | | | | | | | | | |
| | | | | | | | | | |
| | | | | | | | | | |
| | | | | | | | | | |
| | | | | | | | | | |
| | | | | | | | | | |
| | | | | | | | | | |
| | | | | | | | | | |
| | | | | | | | | | |
| | | | | | | | | | |
| | | | | | | | | | |
| | | | | | | | | | |
| | | | | | | | | | |

# Benchmark Tracking Chart

Name ___________________

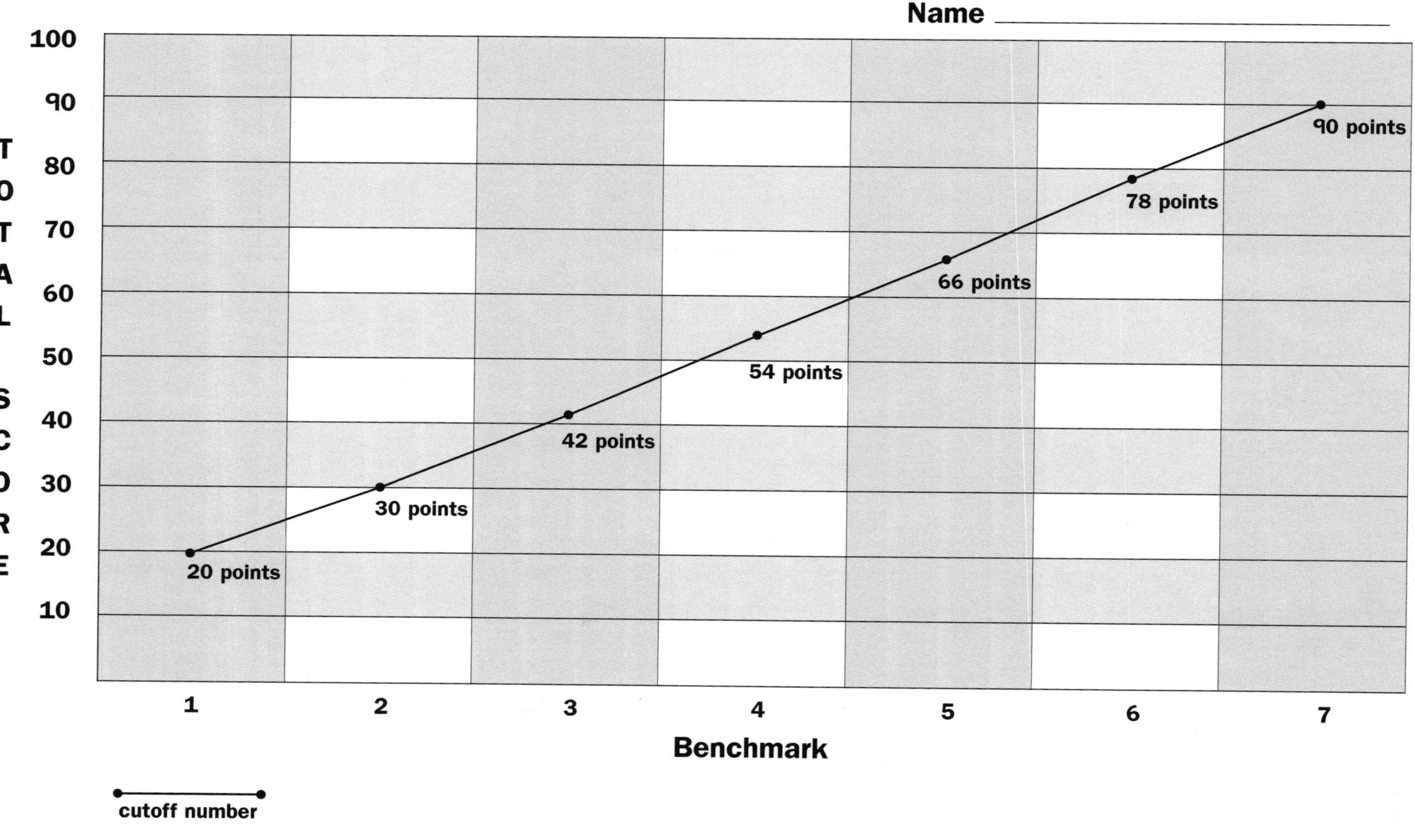